W9-BIA-185

Laughter Keeps You Young

John K. Walker

Printed by:
A & J Printing
P.O. Box 518
Nixa, MO 65714

Published by and order from:
John A. Walker
530 Alger Ave.
Manistique, MI 49854
Phone: 906-341-2082

Library of Congress Cataloging-In-Publication Data   ₮
Walker, John A.

ISBN 0-9639798-1-7

2nd Printing

John A. Walker writes for:
White Pine Publishing Inc.
212 Walnut St.
Manistique, MI 49854
Phone: 906-341-5200
(Manistique Pioneer Tribune)

©All Rights Reserved, including the right to reproduce this book or any portions there of in any form without the approval of John A. Walker.

These stories are written to show the humorous side of working as a Game Warden - living in Michigan U.P. They are not meant to offend anyone and are just the writers version of the stories as he heard or saw them. No names are used in the stories without prior approval.

I dedicate this book to my four kids, Johnny, Robert, Rhonda, Cathy, who gave me all my gray hair. (but they did put up with all dad's flaky ideas) and to all the youth I came across in all the recreational safety classes throughout the years.

Builder of Bridges for Him
W.A. Dromgoole

An old man, traveling a lone highway,
Came at the evening cold and gray,
To a chasm vast and deep and wide.

The old man crossed in the twilight dim,
The sullen stream held no fears for him,
But he stopped when he reached the other side,
And built a bridge to span the tide.

"Old man," said a fellow pilgrim near,
"You are wasting your strength with building here,
Your journey will end with the ending of day,
And never again will pass this way.

"You have crossed the chasm deep and wide.
Why build you a bridge at eventide?"
And the builder raised his old gray head;
"Good friend, on the path I have come," he said,
"There followed after me today
A youth whose feet will pass this way."

"This chasm which has been as naught to me,
To that fair-haired boy may a pitfall be;
He, too, must cross in the twilight dim,
Good friend, I am building this bridge for him.

The U.P.
Upper Michigan

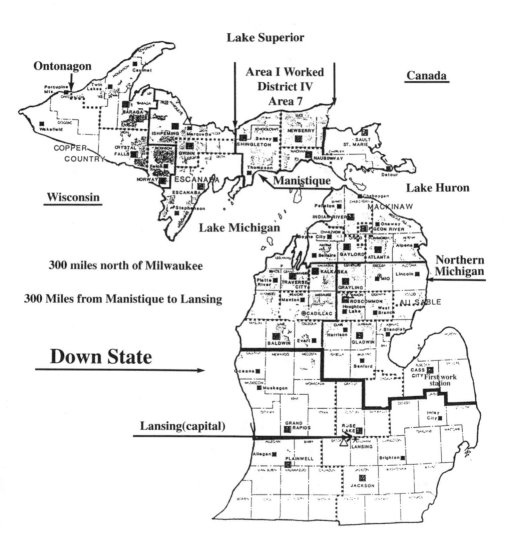

INDEX

Plus, a U.P. Backwoods Glossary-Append.

The Pictures: This book contains a number of old logging and hunting pictures from my dad's stuff, along with some I picked up at yard sales. Needless to say, I did not take them and do not know who did, so I cannot take credit for taking them. If you like old pictures of the U.P. you will like these. A number had Diamond Lumber Company written on the back.

THE COVER

I dedicated this book to my kids, who have always been Dad's best fans even when deep, deep down they may have wondered about him. The picture on the cover of this book is from an oil painting that a friend of my oldest boy did. It is one of those gifts that all the kids had a part in that money could never buy.

The man that painted this picture (John Holbach) from Pensacola Christian College, where a couple of my kids went, is a commercial artist and really good. I cannot believe the detail that some artists can put into an oil painting. You can read the badge, name tag, and shoulder patches.

The fawn in this picture was seized from a party that had it illegally, and the picture was taken in the back room at the Michigan State Police Post here in Manistique. The artist put in all the background and details to make it look like an outdoor scene. (Really there was a breath-alizer machine over my right shoulder.)

Conservation Officer's Stories,
Upper Michigan Tales from a Game Warden's perspective.

"A BUCKET OF BONES"

FORWARD

This is the second book of this type I have put together. The first one
titled "A Deer Gets Revenge" was done on a wing and a prayer.
Whenever a person takes a chance on something, they may hope, but
they never really know how things will turn out. The first of October,
1993, I received a shipment of 5,000 copies of "A Deer Gets Revenge".
From a standing start in my garage till the 1st of the year, I sold basically the first printing of 5,000 copies. There was no way in my greatest
dreams that I ever thought I would sell more than my goal of 500 books
by Christmas. I had a lot of help from a lot of great people: From Buck
LeVasseur of "Discovering" on TV 6 out of Marquette, Michigan, to
dozens of newspaper reporters that did not know me from Adam, but
liked the book so ran an article on it, to business people that took a
chance and put it in their stores to try to sell a few copies for me. Then
there were the radio talk show people that let me get on their programs
to say something about my book, plus Ken from a radio station in
Escanaba here in the U.P. that gave me some help along with some
pointers when I first started out. My hat goes off to all these people and
a   heartfelt "Thank you".

First, let me say that there are a couple things in this book that are a
spin-off from "A Deer Gets Revenge". First of all, the map in the front
is the same, so those that are not lucky enough to live in the U.P. can
understand where we come from. Second, the U.P. BackWoods
Glossary is expanded in this book. I have to put this in the book,
because my sister, Judy, who is a schoolteacher down near Milwaukee,
Wisconsin, claims we use terms up here nobody else in the world ever
heard of. This glossary is to help out those who have a lesser understanding of the English language.

These stories, too, are from my weekly "Fish Report" (that usually has
little or nothing to do with fishing) that is printed in the Manistique
Pioneer-Tribune. They are all "true" but have a little U.P flavor to the
telling of them. It is meant to be a humorous book so a person can come

home, kick their shoes off (in the middle of the floor) and sit and relax while reading it. The only guarantee is that it will not tax your brain too much to understand it.

One of the mysteries of why my other book sold so well may be the following paragraph found in the forward of it. Schoolteachers, business people, and others told me this was one of the keys.

"One thing you will notice about this book is that there are not any "bad" words used in it. Maybe some bad English, but not any bad words. For you see, I grew up in the era of a bar of Fels-Naptha soap for boys if you used one of these words that are so common on TV and in everyday life today. I wanted something that even young kids could sit, read, and get a laugh out of without having to hide it between the box springs and mattress of their bed. Besides, I still have bad dreams of that dull red, green, and dirty-white soap wrapper when those words slipped out around Mom and Dad." I don't know if what I have been told is true- that this is what helped sell the book-but I do not think humor has to be dirty to be funny. Sometimes just telling the truth is funny enough.

The Cross-Cut Cafe here in the U.P. is in the middle of that famous place called "The Middle of Nowhere". The owner of the Cross-Cut Cafe told me, "John, I don't know what you have going for you, but it is the best thing that happened to me. Usually this time of the year, after the color season and before deer season, things really slow down. But with the sales of your book, there have been enough people stop by for it and eat that it has been good for you but great for me." What could I say? I was not selling the book; it was selling itself.

I had a dream when I retired of setting up a scholarship fund for the youth from the school that my kids attended. I placed some money in this fund when I retired and made a promise while putting the book together that if it sold I would put $1.00 from each book into it. My goal was to sell 500 books in the last three months of 1993, but I made another promise that if there were over 4,000 copies sold during the first three months I would start giving out scholarships in January of 1994. Needless to say, I was able to keep both promises.

I wanted people out there to realize that those of us that like to hunt and fish and enjoy the great outdoors also love the youth that we come in contact with. We are not the big jerks that some people would like to portray.

Plus, as a bonus, you will get to meet Eino and Teivo in this book. These are my two fictitious caricatures from the Copper Country that get talking together. Really, sometimes Eino and Teivo (and myself) think there is more wisdom at Plutchak Brothers Garage in Mass, MI, then there is in both Lansing and Washington combined. More world problems are solved there and other coffee shops around the U.P., with better answers, then those down at the BIG House trying to solve them for us. Most of these U.P. people have been through the school of hard knocks, and many have even taken a graduate course or two in it. They have their own ideas about things and how come they happen the way they do and maybe, sometimes, how they think they can be corrected. But, most of the time, they just get a kick out of those poor unfortunate souls that have to spend their life living outside the great U.P.

Remember when reading about these two, they go through life with one great philosophy, "If you take two halftruth, and put them together, you must have the whole truth because everyone knows two halves make a whole."

Chapter 1
Mom Said There Would Be Days Like This!

I don't care where you go as a Game Warden you have to listen to people that have their Game Warden story to tell. The teller may be a state legislator, a gas station owner, a little corner store owner, or someone in a cafe when you stop for lunch. Everyone likes to tell an outdoor story, especially when it's one they figure "stuck" the Game Warden. Here are a few I have heard around the country. Some may be true, some may be part true, and some may be what someone wished was true.

Not Her

I was talking to this state legislator in the courthouse one day, and he just had to take time to tell me one of his favorite stories. It seems that back in the area where he lived there was this Conservation Officer he knew (I worked with him and knew him, too). This officer was always sharp-looking and thought everything out before he jumped into anything. He was an excellent officer and well respected in his work area.

One time this Game Warden went out and managed to catch a party with an illegal deer. It was not an accident-type deal where a person shot an illegal deer by mistake. This guy, if he was caught with it, probably had it coming. The only problem was, the way the story was told to me, this outlaw had the deer at his house already when he got caught with it. So, the officer confronted him about the deer. Now remember that in Michigan, if you get caught with an illegal deer, you lose your hunting rights for about three years. All these guys that get caught hate this part of the law. So, this man of the house got to thinking as the officer was talking to him about the illegal deer and came up with a plan!

"Officer, that's not my deer, it belongs to my wife!" Now what is the officer to do? There is nobody to tie him to the deer, and both of them are living in the house, so both have "their rights" as to what comes and goes at the house. Oh well, if that illegal deer belongs to the lady of the house, I guess she will have to go to court and answer for it. But really everyone knew who the illegal deer belonged to.

Now you have to picture this, as the legislator told it to me. Here is this big, sharp officer going into court with this lady who has supposedly just shot an illegal deer and dragged it home. This may not have been too bad except that she walks into the courthouse about nine plus months pregnant! Big as a lady of her condition could be! She stood there with a straight face and claimed she had been the one to have the deer at her house.

O' Those Dark Nights

When I first started working as a Game Warden, I worked with a couple of ex-Detroit police officers. These two alone could cause a young officer serious brain damage. The one in these couple of short tales was a great big guy that always had a smile on his face.

One night he was out working illegal deer hunters. This officer was working a farm area where we usually found a farm lane and backed up in it to hide our car from the spotlighters that would work the area. On this night he was working by himself and had been out for quite a while. He decided to back down this lane far away from any houses and just sit and wait to see if anyone came along shining for deer.

He figured he must have dozed off, for all of a sudden, something struck him on the back of his neck! It felt hot and moist! He slowly put his hand back there and felt something warm and thick, and all he could think of was that he was bleeding! He reached down for his flashlight and shifted his eyes to see what his hand looked like and what was on it and what damage had been done to his neck!

As the beam of his flashlight went over his shoulder, he about jumped through the roof of the car! For right at his shoulder was a big old milk cow that had reached her nose through the window and blown hot, slimy, wet, sticky mucus (snot) all over his neck!!

Things have to get better, right? Not Always! This same officer one other time was out on night patrol (maybe, he should give these night patrols up). In the area where he worked there were big, deep drainage ditches for draining the farm fields. Some of these could be ten to twelve feet deep.

As I have said in other stories, back in those days, a Game Warden might leave his house after dark and drive around for hours without ever using his headlights while looking for violators. On this night this officer, the same ex-Detroit police officer, was driving down this gravel road without any headlights looking for shining activity. He had covered a few miles and made this turn to head down a gravel road to check some fields. All of a sudden, his car jerked and bounced and came to a sudden stop! The drive wheels were still going around, but the car was stationary. He reached down and turned on his headlights and SUR-PRISE! Here this officer sat with half his car almost on the road and the other half (the passenger side) hanging over the edge of about a ten foot deep drainage ditch. He figured, "Oh, well. I might as well get out and figure out what to do." So he started to slide out the door, but as he did, the car started to tip over more and more into the drainage ditch that was full of water. A couple of times he tried to get out but found that the only thing that was keeping his car from rolling over into the ditch was his weight. Finally he had to swallow his pride and reach down to get the radio, then call the state police post for help, knowing full well that it might be easier to jump out and let the car fall into the ditch than put up with the troopers when they got there and saw what a predicament he was in.

But, Mom, You Said . . .

When you are a Conservation Officer you have a million and one policies to live by. When you start, they give you a truck load of looseleaf binders with all the rules for all occasions. One rule you have to live by is that if you are not wearing a tie, you have to wear a V-neck T-shirt that does not show. So, most officers have a number of these to wear with their uniforms. Now, as you can tell, I grew up in the great U.P. I learned from my Mom the importance of doing things for myself. If the wife is busy and you want something done, just go ahead and do it. So I did.

I was going out later in the day goose hunting with one of the teenagers I take hunting with me. That morning I was looking over my uniforms and checking things out. I noticed that my V-neck T-shirts were not as white as they used to be, so I figured I would wash them with a little bleach and clean them up. Now, I knew that the women when whites get a little dingy would pour some bleach into the wash water, and according to the TV ad, they come out looking like new. This I did. In fact, I figured as long as I was doing it I might as well whiten up all the underwear I had, except what I had on. I took all I owned out of my dresser and put them into the washer. Then I poured in the bleach and let the washer fill up. I then shut it off and let it sit for awhile and turned it back on when I went out and picked up my buddy to go hunting.

We had a great day and both got our limit of geese. When we got back home, he called his parents to come and see what we had gotten. When they came over, we took the geese down to the basement to clean them. While down there, I figured I may as well throw my T-shirts into the dryer and get that project done. I opened up the top of the washer, looked in, and thought, "O'man! How did all that toilet tissue get into the washer with my underwear?!" As I leaned over, I saw that this wasn't toilet tissue but my underwear!! That is what was left of it!! I did a study, without even knowing it, and found that the only thing that survives if you dump about two gallons of bleach into a washer with your underwear is the T-shirt neck band and the elastic waistband from the shorts!! BUT, the little pieces of tissue-like material were really white!

My Turn

There were two officers that always worked together and got along great. In the U.P. it is nothing to have to travel around 100 miles to get to an area where you have to work. The other thing is, there are not too many Hardee's in most of the areas where we ended up working. In fact, usually there are not even any restaurants at all. Of those there are, about half close down for the winter. For this reason, it was normal for an officer to bring a lunch on his long-day journey. When these two officers went out, usually the same officer brought the lunch. He was pretty squared away and had most things figured out pretty well, so you could depend on a good lunch when he brought it.

These two Game Wardens had been working the backwoods area off Lake Superior in the Grand Marais area for a number of nights in a row. There are a number of rivers up here where there are some great steelhead runs in the spring of the year. In fact, much of this area is now part of a federal park, Pictured Rocks National Area. In most of these areas, you either walk back in and hide hoping to catch someone after the steelhead, or you have learned where there is a good spot to hide a car where you can watch for activity. For most of these nights, the younger officer had brought the lunches, cold-cuts sandwiches. After he had brought them two-three days in a row, the older officer said he would bring a lunch for the next night. (Now, this officer was famous as a true old-fashioned Game Warden for the way he operated and did things.) For this reason, the younger officer had his druthers when he offered to bring the lunch, but what could he do?

The next night they were parked in an area, sitting in their car in full dress uniform, watching for some illegal fishing. After they had been there for awhile, the older officer figured it was time for lunch, so he got his bag of goodies out. He told his younger partner to hold out his hand. Now all this was going on in the pitch dark, middle of the night, while sitting in a patrol car. Onto the younger officer's hand, he placed a slice of bread. Now our younger officer figured, this is not bad, maybe we'll have some cold-cuts after all. WRONG! As he sat there holding a slice of bread over his lap, his partner messed around a minute, then reached over and dumped half of a can of pork and beans onto the slice of bread!! Now here he sat in the patrol car, with his hands (for some reason when something starts to leak through your fingers you place your other hand under your first hand) full of soggy bread, soaked with juice from pork and beans running through his fingers onto his lap and seat. His old buddy says, "Good, ain't it?"

Chapter 2
Gifts From Heaven

There are always those, whether they be Game Wardens or poachers, that like to think that it is their skill that leads to catching someone or something. This is not always true. Sometimes the fact that the Game Warden caught someone has nothing at all to do with his skills. In fact, I have come to call these "Gifts from Heaven". I tell people that I am not sure that the Good Lord does not look down and get tired of seeing this poacher get away with his violating all the time, so he just drops him into the officer's lap. These are some of those stories. Some of these people are those that officers had pulled their hair out trying to catch.

A Bad Time for an Accident

One day I happened to be at the Michigan State Police Post when a call came in. It seemed that there had been an accident involving two cars on US-2 in town near the bridge crossing the Manistique River. I got into my patrol car and went over to the area of the accident. The two cars involved were still there, and the people from the vehicles were talking to a couple of the city police officers. One of the officers pointed out into the middle of US-2 and told me I should look at the number of packages wrapped with white freezer paper that were laying all over the road. I went out there, and what did I find but packages of venison laying all over the road. The packages had spilled from one of the vehicles when the wreck occurred. This was not good seeing that it was August and deer season was not open. In fact, it had closed back on January 1st, and it would not open for this year for six weeks yet. I went and talked to the party that had been driving the car (that now nobody claimed to have been driving). He had no idea how all these packages could have come flying out of the car he was not driving at the time of the accident.

We did end up going to court on this case, and with the help of some witnesses that placed the mystery driver behind the wheel, he was convicted.

Just the Right Timing

One night we were out working an area twenty miles north of town. It was out in the middle of the Hiawatha National Forest, so there were no houses for miles. We had been patroling for a couple of hours when I decided to pull into a jackpine plantation and try to hide the patrol car. I hid it all right! I backed over a dead-furrow and really got stuck. In fact, we could not move the car any way but forward with all the trees around it. I had one of these big four foot jacks that would pick up the whole car if you placed it under the trailer hitch. We spent well over an hour jacking the patrol car up and placing pieces of trees and stumps under the back wheels trying to get out. The other officer and myself were both sweating like mules, and it was not a warm night. Finally, we got the back end jacked up and built up high enough to clear the brim of the rut. I got in and went for it! Out we came, back on the 2-track trail. I shut the lights off, we threw our jack and other gear back into the trunk, and sat on the hood having a cup of coffee trying to cool off.

Now we were sitting in the pitch dark when, all of a sudden, a vehicle came flying down this gravel road to stop just a couple hundred feet down the road from where we sat! It was there only a couple minutes when this second vehicle came flying up behind it and some people jumped out yelling, "Conservation Officers!! Don't anybody move"! My partner and I looked at each other knowing this could not be, because we were who they claimed to be. We just sat there as they laughed about their joke and had a beer. The back vehicle then backed up, spun around, and left. The crew from the front car then got back in their vehicle and started off. After going only a couple of feet, they started to shine the opening in the jackpine on the opposite side of the road from us. Nothing was spotted there, so they turned the spotlight to our side of the road.

HERE they did spot something! Two Game Wardens in a marked patrol car! Off they went as fast as they could with us right behind them. All of a sudden, a rifle came flying out of the car to land on the road. They then went a couple hundred yards farther down the road and stopped. We got out, the other officer walked back and got the rifle, and we wrote them out tickets for attempting to spotlight deer. As we were doing this, they gave us a good russing and let us know what they thought of us. I told my partner, "As soon as I give them their tickets, get in the car fast, so we can get out of here." I had noticed one thing.

Now, remember, we were miles and miles from anybody. I had noticed all the time the two vehicles were parked, plus with the use of the spotlight, plus all the time they were giving us the hard time, that their headlights were on and had become this funny yellow color. I wanted to get out of there before they tried to start their car, found out it wouldn't, and asked us to help them. If asked, we would have needed to. They didn't ask, so off we went - fast.

A couple days later we heard the story about the guys who got caught on the 8-mile. After they got their tickets, they got in their car to leave and it would not start; the battery was too run down. They walked all the way out to M-94 and about five miles down 94 before they met a car. They flagged it down and talked the people into taking them back and giving them a jump to start their car. This they did, and their car started right off. The other car left, and they pulled their car into gear. AND it stalled. They walked the ten miles they had already walked once that night and then some before they found help this time.

What's For Supper?

In every town where there are those that are willing to take a deer illegally, there are a hundred stories for each deer they do take. A Game Warden always hears, "So-and-so got a barn full of deer!" I used to always say, "The barn couldn't be full because I just drove by while the doors were open, and I did not see any deer." But needless to say, the stories about certain people go on and get bigger all the time.

One day I received a tip that one of these people that I had heard story after story about (and had caught doing a couple of things) had a deer in his basement! I checked with the party who gave me the tip and got all the information I could. It seemed like he knew what he was talking about. I went out by the house and got a description and the information to try and get a search warrant. Now, if you have ever gotten a search warrant, you would know it is not a five minute project. In fact, a lot of times you are talking a couple of hours. By the time you convince the prosecutor that you have a valid tip and the information is good, you can kiss an hour goodbye. Then there has to be an affidavit typed up. After this, the search warrant itself is typed up. Then you have to find a local judge to swear before and sign the needed papers. Finally, after most of the afternoon, you meet your partner and off you go to serve the search warrant. By this time, the afternoon is shot, and it is supper time.

We head out of town, turn off on the road the party lives on, and head down his gravel driveway. As we pull up in front of the house, the party named on the search warrant is out in the front yard. He sees us coming, but we are there before he can do anything. We get out of the car and walk up to where he is standing and tell him that we heard there was an illegal deer at his house. As he looks the papers over, we keep an eye on the reason he was in the front yard. It seems, seeing it was supper time and a nice warm August day, that it was a good time to barbeque. As the smoke rose off the grill, I asked him what was for supper and if we could have a look. You guessed it! Talk about good timing. There were the illegal deer's tenderloins we were looking for right in the front yard. On the grill getting cooked for supper! Another gift from heaven given to us. I hate to admit it, but we had to take his supper and leave.

Don't Steal My Chair!

There was this day that one of the other officers working in the same town as me received a complaint about an illegal deer being shot. It was after dark, so he went out and picked up the deer and looked around as best he could. The next morning he called me, and we both went out to see what we could find. Neither one of us had much hope of catching anyone with all the hunters in the area, but it was worth a try.

We went into the hemlock where he had recovered the deer and started to backtrack the deer. After a while, we came out on a power line in some real hilly country. We saw a large blood spot, and from the looks of things, this was where the big doe had stepped out into the opening of the power line and been shot. We looked the area over well and could not find a thing. We then tried to figure out where the shot could have come from. We looked off to the west and saw that you could cross a creek and then go up on top of a higher hill about 4-5 poles down. We worked our way toward that point looking for tracks and watching for any signs other than some footprints on the power line.

We got to the area about four power poles down, and from there you had a perfect view of where the big doe had stood. I looked over at the base of the power pole, and would you believe it, there was a little homemade stool sitting there. Big deal, a stool without a body would not do us a whole lot of good! We looked around and even found an empty casing, but we still did not have a person to check out. I walked over to the base of the pole and picked up the stool to take with us. I figured if nothing else, this violator was going to be missing a stool when he came back! I turned it over, and would you believe it, he had his stool fixed so nobody could steal it! He had written his name and address on the bottom of the stool. About this time, my partner found where some tracks left the power line and went out toward the road. We followed them and came to a hunting camp made from an old house trailer. We walked up and asked if so-and-so was around. (I still wonder what he thought when we first called him by name.) We told him what we had and that we had found the stool that he had so graciously written his name on. After a minute, he told us the whole story and confessed to shooting the deer.

Chapter 3
A Bucket of Bones

I guess just about every town has some people that are talked about as being the great outwitter of the Game Warden. If these people were to shoot all the deer and take all the fish told in the stories, there would not be any left to hunt and fish. The subject of this story is one of those guys. He came from a large family that through the years had story after story told about them. Only the good Lord knows how many were true and how many came from the bar or coffee shop. This guy and I always had mutual respect for each other. I had caught a number of his kin, some of them a number of times, but had never really come across him doing anything big. As you read this story, you will see that this may just be one of those that was just meant to be.

Would You Believe?

On this fall night we had made plans to have a group patrol. We were going to have three-four patrol cars working the area, then have the airplane up to spot shiners for us. This was one of the most effective ways to catch those out after dark shining deer. With the hundreds of square miles of area we have to work, with all the main roads, gravel roads, and 2-track roads that cover the area, the plane was one of our best tools.

On this nice clear fall night, I was assigned to work an area called Fletcher Hill. This is some wild land owned mostly by the state and a big papermill company. There are a number of oak ridges in the area with miles of 2-tracks. On this night I was driving a Ford patrol car and it was not made for 2-track travel. As the plane was trying to put me onto a vehicle back in the Fletcher Hill area, I bottomed out so hard with the front end that I bent the radiator. It was not leaking yet, but I figured I had better head back to town and pick up a different patrol unit before I got stranded. I radioed to another officer working closer to town and asked him to go by an officer's house who was not working that night and pick up his patrol car. Then he was to head north on M-94 till we met, and we would switch cars. We met in the area of Adams Road, near Stoney Cut on M-94, and pulled over to switch vehicles. As I was throwing my gear into the other patrol car, out of Adams Road onto M-94 came a vehicle. Back at this time there was only about one person that lived down Adams Road, and she was a lady in her seventies that did not own a car. As the car turned and went by us, I saw it was one belonging to one of the most talked about deer slayers in town. I figured we sure blew this one!

To make matters even worse, while I was at Sunny Shores Restaurant having coffee earlier that same day, a party had come up to me and said, "Well, you must have missed so-and-so last night, because he was just in the store buying some freezer paper." Well, here I was parked right out in the open with not one but two marked patrol cars as he drove by! I was sure he had to see us. After we got the switch made I told my partner, "There's no use going back up M-94. They saw us, so we may as well go over and work the Cooks area. We went over to Thunder Lake Road and up to an apple orchard and hid our patrol car so we could sit and watch.

We had only been there a little while when the other officer working with me decided to have a cup of coffee and liked to died! We were sitting in the pitch dark as he reached back and got his thermos bottle. He opened it up and poured himself a cup. All this took place in the dark. He placed the top back on the thermos and sat back to take a big swig. As he did he started to choke and gag! After he got done and got his breath back, we found out his "coffee" was not coffee, but whatever his wife had put in to clean out the thermos. He had thought it was all ready to take to work so just grabbed it off the counter figuring it was nice fresh coffee.

Just about the time we got done laughing, a vehicle came by shining. Now, these people shined while driving fast, then if they saw a deer they returned to shoot it. I pulled in behind them without any headlights and followed them about two miles up to a cut-across road. Here, I turned on the spotlights, blue light, and headlights to pull them over. They pulled over to the right and four people were in the car. Would you believe it?! This was the same vehicle that had come out of the Adams Road when we were switching patrol cars. (It goes to show, great minds must think alike, for we both ended up at the same orchard.) I walked up to the driver's side and asked the people to step out of the car. All four of them did, and there was a rifle and some spotlights in the car. The rifle was a bolt action, but the bolt was not in it. While the other officer kept an eye on them, I looked the car over and found a bolt for a rifle in the glove box. I took the rifle and tried to get the bolt in. It just about fit, but not quite. I held the trigger back (on some firearms you have to do this), but still it would not fit. I played with the safety to see if it would fit, almost but not quite. No matter what I did, the bolt would start in but not quite fit. I must have tried for over five minutes when the guy from the front passenger side said, "John, I don't care how hard you try, you will not get that bolt in that gun! This is the bolt for that gun!" He pulled a bolt out of his pocket and handed it to me. I thought the driver, the famous one of the lot, was going to have a heart attack when his cousin handed me the bolt for the rifle.

We checked out the inside of the car and got the rifle, now with its bolt, some shells, and the spotlights. The driver said to me, "John, I should have run on you." He had a 428 Ponatic. It was too late, but I told him to be my guest. We were driving 440 Plymouths back then before they put all the anti-pollution garbage on them, and they would just fly. But that wasn't the key. About then the patrol plane went over us to check out how we were doing. He may have outrun me, but it is hard to outrun an airplane.

I was taking the evidence back to the patrol car while the four subjects were standing behind their car in the headlight of the patrol unit. About this time my partner said, "Ok then, (we all knew each other), let's have a look in the trunk." There was dead silence for a couple of minutes... then, the driver, the leader of the lot, said with all seriousness, "John, would you believe my dog dragged it home?" (Remember what I had heard at coffee that morning?) I said, "Not really." He said, "Well, it was worth a try." He popped open the trunk, and there sat, as big as life, a five- gallon white bucket with all the bones from a deer that had just been butchered!! What a gift! To this day, I cannot figure how we were lucky enough to catch this crew in the first place and then have them still have the parts of the deer they had taken the night before.

It was the first and last time I ever caught this guy. He later told me he quit going out after deer. He said, "If I decide I want some deer meat, I'll have someone bring me some by. It's a whole lot cheaper that way."

Just a footnote: This guy was really funny to talk to. He figured it was cruel and inhumane the way they kept making the shining laws tougher and tougher. When I started, you could have a gun in the car with you, but were not supposed to shoot a deer with it. Be real! Then the law went to where you could not have a gun in the passenger part of a car, but it had to be locked in the trunk. We usually stopped vehicles that had the trunk key already in the lock for quick access. Then the law went to where anywhere in the vehicle you could not have the means to kill a deer in any way while you were out shining. Later they changed the law to where you could not shine after 11:00 pm any time of the year and not during November at all. He thought this was going too far, for remember, it had always been a way of life with them. The son of the passenger that had handed me the bolt was caught by a newer officer in the same field around ten years later with two illegal deer in his vehicle. Some things just are slow in changing.

Chapter 4
The Big Buck

Blaney Park is an area along US-2 about twenty miles east of Manistique. It was at one time one of the most famous resorts in the country. They had their own golf course before most places did. They had their own railroad running into the resort and, later, their own landing strip for airplanes. Movie stars, royalty, and many famous people came to Blaney Park Resort. To the west of Blaney to River Road,there is an area of thousands and thousands of acres of wild land. This is made up of marsh, ridges, creeks, and is a jungle to hunt. Along the east side of this area is farm land and a saw mill operation where they cut a lot of cedar in the winter. Inside this area, there are rumors that some of the big bucks live. Now with almost all of it being private land, you know what goes through the minds of those that are not supposed to hunt it. "That's where the monster buck lives, and if only I could get a chance at him!!" Sometimes there are those that are tempted beyond what they are capable of resisting. This is one of those stories where a "BIG" buck came out of the swamp to an area where he was spotted. (The buck on the cover of "A Deer Gets Revenge".)

The Big Buck of North Gulliver Road

One day I was getting gas for my patrol car at the State Police Post in Manistique when a complaint came into the post. There had been a buck shot illegally at the end of North Gulliver Road. (It was into December, and rifle deer season was over, but muzzleloading rifle and bow season were open). I got into a patrol car with the post commander, and off we went.

When we got to the area, we met the property owner that had called in the complaint. He informed us about this big buck that had been hanging around one of his back fields. It seems that all during the rifle deer season there were those that had shined trying to get a shot at it. (Back then you could shine during November, but now you cannot in Michigan.) The buck was too smart and hung out way back on the edge of the field next to the woods. He told us that there were three guys involved, the driver of the vehicle, and two that actually went after the deer. He said the vehicle with the driver had left the area toward Gulliver, but the two other men were still out in the woods on his property.

By this time there were a number of other law enforcement people in the area to help us out. Some staked out the area of a big gas pipeline that runs through the property. (This cut the area where the two men were into a big triangle.) There was snow on the ground so the property owner took me back to the area where he had spotted the two after the big buck. He told me that he had heard some shots and was sure they had hit the deer. We cut across an open field back to the woods. Here there was a skid trail that the property owner, who also cut cedar, took me back on. We worked our way through the swamp back to the pipeline and then picked up the tracks of the two trespassers who were after the deer.

There was snow on the ground, so we followed their tracks till we came to an area where they had found where the deer had dropped after shooting it and were now dragging it. There were two sets of footprints, one on each side of the drag mark. At this time I had no idea what kind of a deer had been shot, other than that it was a buck. We followed this drag mark for over a half mile as they were trying to keep in the woods while working their way out to the edge of the road so their buddy in the vehicle could pick them up. As we walked, I was looking down to keep an eye on the tracks when I glanced up. Down the cedar swamp we were walking in, all I saw laying on the snow was buck antlers!! They had either heard us or seen something that spooked them, so they left the deer and took off toward the pipeline. It was one of those bucks that was all antlers, no size to the deer itself, but what a rack!

When they came to the pipeline, they were spotted by some of our help and caught. We came up with a 5mm rifle and two subjects. The Michigan State Police Crime Lab at Marquette tied this caliber gun into the fatal shot that had killed the big buck. I took the buck to my house for safe keeping and locked it in my garage.

That night someone broke into the DNR garages out at Thompson looking for the deer. In fact, the next morning I found tracks around my house and garage where someone had tried to look in and find the deer to steal the evidence. This is why in the picture we have of the deer, it's on the back of a patrol car up at the District Office in Newberry. We moved it there for safe storage.

One of the funny things about this case is that it was during muzzle-loading season, and this buck could have been shot legally from that standpoint. They still would not have had the right to trespass on private property when hunting, but the buck itself would have been killed legally.

The two that were actually out dragging the deer had to pay for the error of their way, but the driver got off.

Just a side note: There was so much activity in this area after these deer that one time in December, after the close of firearm deer season, we put the airplane up to try and catch shiners, and there were over fifteen tickets issued that one night for illegal hunting. The deer also migrate through this area, and some even spend the winter in the cedar swamps in this large section of wilderness. It was a busy place when I moved to the Manistique area right around 1973-74.

Pictures of Dad's success

Chapter 5
Working in My Garden

Most people like to get out during the first nice warm days of spring and work in their garden. Up in this country, most Game Wardens do not look forward to getting to work in their Garden during the spring of the year. If you look at the map of Michigan in the book, you will see a peninsula going down into Lake Michigan just west of Manistique and south of Thompson; this is the famous Garden Peninsula. The east side of the Garden Peninsula borders Big Bay De Noc which is some of the best fishing area in the country for both perch and walleye. There are only two roads to get down on the Garden Peninsula. One runs south out of Thompson, called Little Harbor Road, and the main black-top road runs south out of Garden Corners on US-2. They both meet down in the town of Garden, and so it is almost impossible to get down on the peninsula to work undetected.

When the ice went out in the spring of the year, the perch would come in to spawn by the tons. It was during this spawning period that most of our problems took place. (There were always those who liked to fish illegally, commercially out in Big Bay De Noc all year round.) Those that were after these fish to sell would use gill nets to take them. I always said that there was more money made during the couple of peak weeks of the spawning runs than anyone made robbing gas stations in Detroit. When you have those trying to take these fish and make the big bucks, add to that the rough spring and fall weather conditions out on the big lake, you have some real potential for serious problems, especially since the work is often done in the dark by both sides. However, there are always those things that take place that bring you down to earth.

These are a couple of stories about working the illegal gill netters off the Garden Peninsula.

A Day on the Big Lake

First of all let me say that working out on the Great Lakes is unique. Where else can you put a boat out on an inland lake, set the automatic pilot, sit back and have coffee, and run for hours?

When I tell tourists up along US-2 in the U.P. that this is the same lake you see south of Chicago and pass in Milwaukee, they give you that funny look like, "You have to be kidding me." Not really. This lake is that big-almost 400 miles by car to travel from the top to the bottom along the shore.

On this day we were out on the lake with a forty foot patrol boat. We had made plans to try and pick up some illegal gill nets that had been set in closed waters. We came from Naubinway to the east of Manistique to the Garden Peninsula area. We had to run for most of the morning (this is at top speed in one of these boats) to just get to the area where the nets were supposed to be. We left before daylight and set our course for the area of the nets. As we were chugging along, there was this older officer sleeping on the engine hatch in the middle of the open back of the boat. Other officers were just sitting around talking to kill time. It is just beautiful out there on a calm day as daylight breaks and the sun rises up out of the lake. You have all read where the fighter planes came out of the rising sun to attack ships during the war? Well, this is what it looks like. You cannot really look into the sun and see anything because it is so bright rising out of the water to the east, or right off the stern of the boat. All of a sudden, out of this ball of fire comes an airplane right off the water to scream over the bow of the boat!! (With all the noise of the boat, we never heard the plane). I swear, if we had looked, we would have found tire marks on the top of the boat's cabin. The old officer that was asleep on the engine hatch went about ten feet in the air and almost ran off the side of the boat into the lake before he realized what had happened. I could just about hear the laughter of our District Pilot as he rose back into the air looking back over his shoulder at the startled crew on the boat.

We finally made it to the area where the nets were supposed to be. We looked around with the aid of Air-4 and located a couple of flags. He set us on a course to get to them and then told us a front was coming in, so he would have to leave. We saw the flag staffs for the nets and swung the boat around to get them on the right side of the vessel to pick them up. As we set a line to go in and grab the flags, the front and the fog hit us like a wall. At one minute it was clear as a bell, then before we could get to the flag, the fog hit. Would you believe it? We never found the flag that was just a couple of hundred yards off our bow. We spent some time trying to locate it but without any luck, so we headed back home.

Now, this does not make my day! You are out in the middle of Lake Michigan in a forty foot boat when you know there are four hundred foot boats running around on the same lake. I have observed some of those forty footers that met a four hundred footer out here, and usually the forty footer lost. The guy running the boat said, "No problem." We would just head for Port Inland and dock there. No problem for him he had grown up as a commercial fisherman and was used to the lake. By now you could not see from one end of the boat to the other, but off we went to somewhere, hopefully Port Inland. The pilot set his controls, got his bearings, and I prayed. We must have run for a couple of hours or more while he joked and laughed, for it did not bother him a bit. All of a sudden, we came out of the fog between the breakwalls of Port Inland. I would like to think the guy running the ship was that good, but it's just hard to do if you ever meet him.

A Bad Day

On one of these famous Garden patrol days, I was assigned to ride with the Post Commander from the state police post in Manistique. Now you have to remember that there is always a good natured rivalry between the Conservation Officers and the State Police. We get along great together, set each other up when we can, and enjoy putting one over on the other when the chance occurs. But, they have never been able to live down the fact that back in the old days when I took the Conservation Officer exam, if you failed to score high enough to qualify to be a Game Warden, you got a letter from the Michigan Department of Civil Service that read something like this. "I'm sorry to inform you that you did not qualify for the job as a Michigan Conservation Officer, but if you are interested in being a Michigan State Trooper, you did qualify for this." What can I say ?

On this day we (DNR law enforcement) were going to make a lasting impression on the Post Commander. We headed out of Manistique to meet the crew from Escanaba District.They started out with three boats they were bringing over by trailer to launch in Garden Bay. When they arrived, they only had two boats with them. It seemed they had left Escanaba with three boats all right, but as they drove east along US-2, one of the boats decided to pull over and pass the patrol car. It is not good when a 17 foot Boston Whaler decides to go out on its own along US-2 at 50-60 miles an hour! The boat did not make the pass, but it did take down a couple mailboxes before it landed in someone's front yard. O'well, on we go with two boats. After all, two are better than none.

They got to the boat landing and launched one boat and were attempting to launch the other one. Now, when you launch a boat from the land into a lake, there is one major objective you have in mind. That is to get the boat you hope to launch TO the lake BEFORE it rolls off the trailer. It does not always work that way and did not on this particular day. The boat launch is kind of, steep, and as they backed down it to the waters edge, the boat rolled off the trailer. It was a perfect launch, only it was about ten feet short of the water's edge. This is not good on the boat or lower unit. They finally got it back on the trailer, but we were down to one boat.

I looked at the Post Commander, and he looked at me. What can I say?

Life goes on in the fast lane. Now, the last boat is already launched, sitting on the edge of Garden Bay with the motor warming up. They had just picked it up from the repair shop the day before, so they were all squared away. It was decided, seeing we were here, that they would take a ride around the bay and look for nets. The rest of the crew got in the boat, and they put it in reverse to back away from the launch. They backed away, and backed away, and backed away!! No matter what they did, they kept backing around and around in circles. The boat would just not shift out of reverse. They tried everything they could think of, but nothing worked. On this day, no one figured it would. Finally the District Supervisor from Escanaba made a great decision, "Load up that last boat! We're going home!"

I always thought if you could have this kind of day with the "elite" people that passed the exam to qualify to be a Game Warden, it's a good thing they don't give those other guys boats.

Feeling Great!

Back in the old days, when commercial fishing was big on the Great Lakes, the Game Warden had to ride with the commercial fishermen from his area a couple times a month. This is not good! First of all, these fish tugs are enclosed with the engine house in the middle. So, you have the fumes from the engine running, plus the smells of a million years of fishing, plus you didn't want to be there in the first place.

Let me say that true commercial fishermen are a tough lot. They get up well before daylight to make their runs. They go out in almost all kinds of weather, out of Manistique, all year around. It is a hard, demanding job. But, it makes their day when a Conservation Officer gets to ride with them.

Let me explain that most gill net tugs in operation at this time were the same ones that Peter and Paul gave up to go with the Lord. They may or may not have had a few repairs and some tin added, but they were rough. Now, a gill net tug sets the nets out the back of the tug through a couple of doors they open off a wheel, but to pick up the nets, the lifter is on the side of the tug. They have what they call a little lifter engine to pull the gill nets in through this opening.

There are two things to remember: One, it was never a nice, calm day when you were assigned to ride these gill net tugs. Two, all these tugs I had to ride had a rounded bottom that would just roll in the waves.

Off we would go with the waves and the smell of fuel and fish to the area they were fishing. They would spot their gill nets and pull along side the staff and pull it in the lifter window. (As I sat in an enclosed area, I could not see the shore or get any fresh air, yet I had my clipboard with reports to fill out.) They would start the lifter motor to add to the fumes and start pulling in the net. You were no longer cutting through the waves when doing this, instead you were basically stopped dead in the water, rolling over the waves crossways in the round bottom boat as they lifted the gill net. Back and forth, back and forth, the fumes from the two engines, the smell of fish, rolling side to side, side to side, the smells, as my complexion started to match the color of my green uniform. All of a sudden, the fishermen found room for me to get some fresh air as I lay over the edge of the boat dying a slow agonizing death as they laughed and thought it was great watching this "kid" get used to a real man's type work.

Chapter 6
The Law of Averages

No matter how hard an officer works, there are times that circumstances just go his way. Through no skill of his own, he catches someone pulling a fast one, and no matter how hard they try to get away, it just doesn't work. These are some short stories along this line.

But, Officer

Now, let me say right off that I was not involved in this case, but someone who I have lived with for almost thirty years tells the story. It seems that down in Missouri where she is from, they have bullfrogs that take steroids. There is a season on these overgrown monsters, but she and others claim that good froglegs are hard to pass up. You don't spear frogs, you gig them. I could never figure out why you gig with a spear in the South and spear with a spear in the North.

Well, on this particular day, Dad and the whole crew of kids were out fishing. I never heard if they caught any fish, but down there you fish with what is called a "doughball". This is Wheaties cereal that you get wet and make into a ball over your hook. Then you cast it out and hope to catch a fish. Remember, the only cereal that will work for "doughballs" is Wheaties.

As they were fishing, they came across a mess of nice, whopping big bullfrogs. Being tempted beyond what they could resist, they took a few. They cleaned them up and had a plan to get them back home, because you see, season on bullfrogs was closed. Everything was going great, and even when they got stopped by the Game Warden, their plan was foolproof!

The Game Warden asked all the usual questions and got all the usual answers. "NO! NO! No! No!" Then the warden asked if they had any bullfrogs. Dad answered with the only answer he ever answered with, "No." The officer was just about to turn away, being satisfied, when the little brother said in all seriousness, "Yes you do, Dad! You hid them right under the Wheaties in the Wheaties box."

It seemed that their foolproof plan was to clean the bullfrogs, dump out the Wheaties from the box, place the froglegs in the box, and put the rest of the cereal back in the box to cover and hide the froglegs. Well, it almost worked!!

The Help of a Tree

When you are a Game Warden in the U.P., you are bound to have some real good rivers for salmon and steelhead runs. If you have these, you are always going to have someone after the fish. My problem was that the river was right here in town, and anybody could just walk down to it. Plus, this river had what they call a flume running down the middle of it. (A wall twelve feet off the water.) Violators would get up on the flume and walk along the edge of it till they saw some big steelhead or salmon and could try to snag them. If they saw a warden, they would just cut their line and let the fish and hook go down the river.

On this day I spotted a couple of our famous fishermen up on the flume wall. I had an unmarked vehicle, so I got down to the area of the flume to watch them without them knowing who it was. One of them finally snagged a big steelhead trout and was playing it along the wall. I moved around hoping to get close enough to grab him before he could cut the line. I waited and he came toward me, but all of a sudden he looked up and spotted me. As he cut the line, it snapped from the strain of the big steelhead. The line whipped down off the flume wall toward the water in the river where suddenly it caught on some tag alder brush growing at the base of the flume! Here was our fisherman watching in horror as the tag alder worked as a perfect pole playing the fish back and forth in the water. I walked over to my patrol unit, as the fisherman watched and took some waders out of the trunk. I walked out in the river and retrieved the illegally hooked fish and the fisherman's illegal hook. Then off we went to court.

Where's An Officer When You Need One?

There was this one other time I was working down in the area of the flume on the Manistique River during the fish runs. I had just left the state police post, and I went down to check the activity on the river. As I pulled in, I saw two brothers that I knew quite well up on the flume wall trying to get some fish. (Now, remember that just being up on the flume wall was a trespassing violation.) As I drove along the old road next to the river, the two brothers spotted me. Off they went running along the flume.

As they ran one way, I would speed up and get to the end before they could get off. Off they would go running for the dam to get off the other end of the flume. I would back up and cut off their escape that way, then off we would go again the other way. Back and forth, back and forth. Finally they got tired, so they sat down right in the middle of the flume. I got out of my patrol car with a camera and took a couple of pictures of them just in case they did get away. I finally got on the radio and called the state police post and asked if the trooper I had been talking to when I gassed up was still there. He was. I asked if he could come down to the river in the area of the dam and cut off two illegal fishermen for me if they ran that way.

He was on his way, so I went down to my end and got ready. All of a sudden there were state police cars and police dogs all over the place!! The two brothers stood up on the flume and could not believe what they were seeing! Dogs, police, more dogs, and more police. Now the attitude was, "OK, take off running", but they didn't. They came off the wall and received their tickets.

It seems that when I called the post and asked if the trooper (singular) was at the post to help me out, half the state police dog handlers from the whole state were a block away at the National Guard Armory setting up to do some dog training. When they overheard the radio traffic, they figured, "Why just practice when we can have the real thing if these two take off running?" Only the illegal fishermen did not feel like cooperating.

Big? Little?

Thompson Creek is a small creek that runs through the little town of Thompson about six miles west of Manistique. This is where the Thompson State Fish Hatchery is located. For this reason, there was a weir for years on Thompson Creek so they could trap and take salmon for their spawn. When the fish would run up the creek to the area of the weir, it stopped them from going any farther upstream. Some people sure found these salmon tempting.

On this particular day, there was a state trooper fishing for salmon off the mouth of Thompson Creek out in Lake Michigan. Back in those days Thompson Creek was closed to fishing altogether; now you can fish it during the normal trout fishing season. As usual, all the fish were in the creek, and those trying to catch them out in the lake were not having much luck. The trooper was walking around when he noticed one of the Thompson natives standing on the weir checking the salmon out. He walked up that way and got close enough to see the party take a big rock and throw it down into the fish laying against the weir. He managed to strike one that came floating up and he had him a big salmon. I was at the Thompson field office, the trooper got ahold of me, and a ticket was issued to this party for taking a fish illegally with a big rock.

Wouldn't you know it? He pled not guilty. I was in court when he appeared and entered his not guilty plea before the judge. The trooper was at home that day and not in court. The judge asked the party, "If we can get ahold of the trooper, the Game Warden is here, would you want your trial today before me?" The fish-taker said that would be all right, so I went and called the state trooper at home. He told me he would be there in about a half hour.

During this time the judge, the defendant, and myself were sitting in the courtroom talking. Like I say, in the U.P. everybody knows everybody else. We were still waiting on the trooper. The judge told our party, "Now, you don't have to answer this if you don't want to, but let me ask you. Did you take a fish with a BIG rock?" The party sat for a minute thinking then said, "No! It was a little rock."

The judge then asked, "Would you be interested in pleading guilty to taking a fish illegally with a little rock?" Without batting an eye the party said, "Yes!" So he pled guilty to taking a salmon illegally with a little rock, paid his fine, and left the courtroom happy as could be.

The judge looked at me with that certain look in his eye, threw up his hands, and with a shrug of his shoulders said, "I guess big or little is all in the eyes of the beholder." Case closed.

One Answer Too Many

One day I was checking ice fishermen out on McDonald Lake. I came up on a whole crew of young men fishing. As I checked licenses, I counted poles to see how many were there. I had observed a couple of the guys pulling up lines and checking for fish, but others were just standing around. One of the young men I saw using a couple tip-ups told me he was just 16 years old. (In Michigan you do not need a fishing license to fish til your seventeenth birthday) I knew he was lying to me because I remembered him from school. He was the same age as my two boys. I looked things over and gabbed with them all the time trying to figure out how to find out how old he was. No luck.

As we were talking, one of the boys brought up the fact that they would like to get one of those summer jobs working for the DNR. I told them about the jobs and that they would have to go out to the office and apply for them. The party whom I had seen with the tip-ups, who now was an old sixteen, asked who he should see out there. I told him to just go to the field office at Thompson and ask Bev for a form and fill it out. Then real quick I said, "But remember you have to be over 17 to apply for the jobs with the state!" Our fishing buddy said, real fast without engaging his brain, "That's no problem. I'm nineteen." All I heard from his buddies on the ice was laughter and "Dummy, dummy, dummy." He had that "Oh, No" look on his face.

Chapter 7
Now Boys, Dad Knows Best

There are always those times as dads go through life raising teenagers that what they say or do comes back to haunt them. It may be with the best of intentions and a ton of thought that they make a decision, but the end results are not always what Dad had in mind. I have been there and so have you if you raised teenagers, so you know what I am talking about. Here are a number of stories along this line.

O'Christmas Tree, O'Christmas Tree

Up here in the good old U.P. it is usually a family project to go out and get a Christmas tree. You can get a permit from the National Forest Service to cut one, or some private owners may let you take one, or you may even go to a Christmas tree farm. As Christmas rolls around, you pack up the family. In this case, the family was a couple teenage boys loaded into the GEO (this is a car, maybe). Off they went. Since they didn't own a pickup, they just took some rope, a saw, and headed out to get a tree. Remember, if you are originally from Ontonagon and have a degree from that university up in Marquette, where there's a will, there ought to be a way with Dad in charge.

Now, if you are a true Yooper, you want a tree that goes all the way from the floor to the ceiling. There is no such thing as a table top tree till you get so old you have to spend the winters in Florida. You go out and look over a whole lot of trees til you find the one that's just what you need. You check it out from all sides to make sure and then saw it down. It is definitely a floor model and should fill up the living room if you can get it home. "No problem," Dad says as he and the two teenage boys throw it up on the roof of the GEO (almost a car). Mom is standing by watching to make sure her tree is not hurt. As it is being held on the roof, Dad starts to tie it down with the rope. Around the tree a couple of times, over the side, around this tie-down, back over the tree to the other side, through that tie-down, back over the tree once again, tie it to a tie-down once more, then back over one last time and tie it down to the tie-down for the last time!

Dad looks the job over with Mom standing there nodding her head and the teenage boys knowing Dad sure has his act together. "All right," Dad says, "Into the car and let's head home." Ok, into the car. Into the car? Into the car! But how? The only things Dad had to tie the rope to were not tie-downs after all, but the door post! With all the rope wrapped around the tree, from door post to door post, they couldn't get any of the doors open to get in!! There has to be a way, but I wonder where the keys are to the car? If they can find them, there may be a way. This Geo has a hatch back. (Oh, for a home video of this!) They get the hatch in the back open.

Then Mom and Dad have to crawl into the car through the back hatch, over the back seat, up to and figure out how to get through or over those front seats that go almost to the roof.

Finally Dad gets between them into the front driver's seat, and they all head for home with Dad saying, "I had it planned like this all the time! It was just a test to see if you boys were watching what I was doing!"

Don't Get Wet

When one of my boys was a teenager, the man he worked for gave him a snowmachine. Really it was almost like new, in real good shape, a two year old Ski-doo. When I would go out on patrol on weekends, he would go with me as I checked fishermen, deer yards, and ran the snowmobile trails. We must have put on thousands of miles together and really had some great times working together. During all these hours and hours out there and the miles and miles we traveled, we never had any real problems with the snowmachines. Except this one time!

This one day we had made a sixty mile circle that ended up on Indian Lake checking ice fishermen. Now, let me explain something to you people that have never ice fished or been out on a lake on the ice. As the ice forms in the cold weather, it is bare and slick as can be. Later in the year as the snow keeps falling, the weight on the ice forces it down and water comes up through what we call pressure cracks. When this happens, you get a mixture of water and snow on the ice. This slush can be two to three feet deep in places, and it is really weird to step in and sink down knowing and hoping there is solid ice under your feet, someplace.

On this day, we had checked a number of fishermen on the north end of the lake, and we headed south toward town. All of a sudden, Rob's machine stopped, and one pull on the rope told me we had a problem. I took the spark plugs out and one look told me, "Bad news." They were pounded just full of aluminum. There was no way to get it running, so the only thing we could do was try to pull it off the lake. This is where all Dad's wisdom came in.

As usual I had along some tow rope that I hooked on the back of my sled and tied to the front of his. Now, we had a half to three-quarters of a mile to go to shore so we could get his machine out to a road. Bob said, "But, Dad." I answered with those famous words all dads say, "Don't worry, son, this will work." You see, my sled was a big 440 and it would just fly. In fact, under the right conditions I could get it up to 85-90 miles an hour. So I figured with the handicap of pulling his machine, I would only be able to get up to about 45 to 50 miles an hour, but this should do. I told him to put on his helmet and hang on, because I was going to wind it up and head for shore. Off we went.

There was only one problem! (We were aware of it, but Dad had it figured out. I thought! It was a couple hundred yards of two foot deep slush between us and the shore.)

So off we went. The rope tightened up, and I gave my machine the gas while looking over my shoulder to see the boy hanging on twenty feet behind me. 10...20...30...40...45 was the best I could do with Mrs. Walker's number two son holding me back. But at this speed, we should be able to clear the slush by flying across the top of it! My machine hit the slush with one big splash, and I was going to make it across! (You notice that "I" is singular.)

When my son's snowmachine hit the slush, my theory fell apart. For without his track spinning, it worked like a brake. The boy and his machine just stopped and started sinking, but my machine with the dragging weight now gone just spun the track and shot out of the slush burying the boy and his machine with water and slush behind me. What a sight! I still laugh typing this story and picturing him with that shocked look on his face.

What a job it was standing in the icewater getting his machine out! Really, Dad's idea was good, it just didn't work.

Now, make sure my wife doesn't read this story because we never told her about this one either.

For Once, Dad Was Right

In December up in the U.P. you can hunt deer with a bow and arrow. Also, very seldom in the northern part of the U.P. do you find a December without snow on the ground. During this story, it was bow season and there was snow on the ground.

Dad and his son were bow hunting, and the boy shot a nice big deer. The deer took off, so the boy went and got Dad to help him track it. (In fact, if you hunt with a bow and hit a deer, it is better to wait a while before you track it to let it lay down and stiffen up.) Dad and the boy came back and got on the track of the deer.

Now, we all know that a deer never runs toward a road when wounded but as far away from any road as it can get. This deer was true to form. Farther and farther they went back into the swamp, away from the road, tracking the deer. With the snow on the ground, there was little or no chance they would lose the deer; it was just a matter of tracking it down.

After going quite a way (always away from the road and their truck), they came upon the deer. It was about done in but still standing. The boy pulled up and got ready to finish the deer off when dad said, "Hold it! You get around behind him on the far side. I'll go around on this side, and let's drive him back toward the road as far as we can. If you finish him off here we'll have to drag him all the way out." Good idea, and it worked! They got the deer back a little more than half way to the road before the deer went down and had to be finished off. See, once in awhile Dad's ideas do work out.

Back When Dad Was A Kid

Remember that famous phrase that you use on your kids and your dad used on you? "Back when I was a kid......" Now, here are some interesting facts about that time. I like to read history, and this is a little information to let you know that some things Dad says may be true. The other day I was reading some history about the old Conservation Department, now the DNR. You may find some of this interesting:

In 1945, spending was to hit $815,000 for fish and wildlife management and their programs. The Conservation Commission also approved a budget of $623,000 for the 1946-47 fiscal year. Of this, fishermen would contribute $220,000 and hunters would add $595,000 to the programs. The commission was also going to ask for legislative approval to charge $1.50 for a trapping license instead of charging a fee on traps. Interesting, it seems back then you paid a fee for each trap you used? It was $1.00 for the first 20 traps and 10 cents for each trap over 20. I bet this was fun for the Game Warden to figure out. During the year 1944 there were 663,322 muskrats taken in Michigan. This was down from 1943 when 995,443 were taken. In April of this year (1944), beaver trappers took 12,068 beaver in the U.P. It was big business back then.

The other thing I read in this article, believe it or not, was a section that had the following headlines, "Smelt Comeback Seen". It read, "Smelt may be staging a comeback in Michigan waters of the Great Lakes, particularly in the waters of Northern Lake Michigan. A mysterious epidemic during the winter of 42-43 greatly reduced the numbers of smelt in the waters of Lake Michigan. Shipments of smelt to the Chicago market were up this year showing the smelt are making a comeback.

The interesting thing is, if a person should read enough history on the type problems we face today, most of them were around sometime before. There is a saying that may fit, "The one thing humans never learn from history is history." Could this be why when Dad says, "Back when I was a kid..." he is just telling the truth as it comes around a second time for him?

Chapter 8
Scared Near To Death

As a Game Warden, there are those times, burned in your memoir forever, that you can sit back and laugh at now, but when they happened they were not really funny. In fact, some were downright scary! This chapter is about some of those crazy things that happen to Game Wardens out working the field. The only thing is that you have to wait til after everyone is retired to tell the stories, because for some reason, they were never included in your Monday morning report to the District office. Some I was there on, in fact most of them, but some are those told in the whirlpool up in Marquette at in-service training. Now, to get the real effect you have to place yourself out there and picture yourself in the middle of some of these situations.

A What?

One night I was working with an officer from the Copper Country. (I should have known I was in trouble). We were working the Inland Quarry area in southeast Schoolcraft County. In this area there are two big, open pit limestone quarries. The rock from the quarry that is inland from Port Inland harbor is transferred to the crusher and harbor by train. The tracks run through the woods for about five miles from the quarry to the harbor. In this same area, without any houses, there are a lot of deer, so needless to say, it can be an active area for poachers. On this night we were working illegal night-time deer hunters.

We would sit awhile, then move around, then we would find another place to sit and wait for some activity. On this particular night, I was a passenger in a pickup driven by this other officer. We had sat awhile and decided to move down Batty Doe Lake Road toward a blacktop road that runs into the area off US-2. As we were moving along slowly without lights (it was one of those super dark nights), we thought we saw some shining going on up to the north of us. We headed up that way, still without headlights on. When we were about a half mile from the blacktop, just before you cross the railroad tracks between the quarries, we thought we saw headlights coming off the blacktop toward us! My partner, the driver, sped up to get down the access road along the railroad tracks before this vehicle turned down Batty Doe Lake Road and saw us. We were going along at a pretty good clip (in the dark, still without any headlights on) when all of a sudden there was something as big as a house right in the middle of the road in front of us I yelled, but it was too late!! As we hit this thing, we went airborne and luckily landed on all four wheels in a state of shock. We were counting all our parts to make sure they were still there.

The truck was still running, so we turned to see what had attacked us. After the driver got out, I had to get out his door, because the front fender on my side was now holding my door shut. We looked to see what we had hit, and here lay a rock--a HUGE rock--that had fallen off one of the trains into the middle of the road. We checked the patrol truck out, and believe it or not, it was not as bad as it could have been (which tells you nothing about how bad it was). We then checked the rock that was higher than the top of the hood of the 4x4 pickup, and we had not even hurt it. In fact, there was just a little green paint and a scrape mark where we bounced over it. Thank goodness it was a glancing blow and not head-on, but our nerves were done for the rest of that night patrol.

It's Funny Now

I have worked with some interesting officers in my days, and the one in this story was an all-state athlete. It was a good thing. On this early spring day we were out walking on snowshoes (the snow was about three feet deep) as we checked for illegally set beaver traps. It was a great day to be alive and outdoors; the sun was shining, and we had been going through a thawing period. We knew where there were some traps set by this trapper that was always good for one or two violations a spring. He was not a bad guy, just never took the time to do things right. So, we figured to walk in and check out some of his beaver sets.

We parked our patrol car, put on our snowshoes, and set off back to the beaver ponds. Now in this area, there were a number of ponds that ran for miles one after another. There were beaver houses on some of the ponds, but in a lot of them were what we called bank beaver. This means instead of having a beaver lodge like we see in the movies, they have theirs built back in the bank. When they do this, they have a small hole that leads back into the lodge. If a trapper wants to improve his odds of catching a beaver, he sets a trap in this hole to get the beaver as they come out. It is illegal to do this.

As we were checking this one pond, I was walking along the bank, and the other officer cut across the pond to check out a beaver hole in the far bank. He was about two-thirds of the way across the beaver pond when the ice gave out and down he went out of sight in the water. (You would have to be standing there and see this happen to know what goes through your mind in that split second. When something like this happens, it is like real slow motion as you watch what takes place, but it all happens in a matter of seconds.) I reached down to take off my Alaskan type snowshoes to try and reach out to the area where my partner went through. But, before I could do much, up he came with two-thirds of his body clearing the hole in the ice, and then he just started rolling over and over for the shore. Man, was I scared, and then was I glad he was such a good athlete in good shape, or else he may not have made it.

What is interesting is that usually after this happens you both just sit and laugh about the past couple minutes. I don't know if it's because of how scared you were and nerves or just because it really is funny as you re-think it after everybody is all right.

Too Mad To Be Scared

In the area where I worked, they had just planted a number of turkeys. I could never figure out why they always seem to plant things, whether they be fish or game, right in the area where the officer has some of his best clients. While on patrol one day, I saw tracks headed back in the snow toward the area where the turkeys had been planted. When I looked into the parked vehicle and saw an empty gun case, I put two and two together and came up with six.

I parked the patrol car and set off back in the woods following these footprints in the snow. I was walking through some jackpine, and the tracks were kind of wandering around in no particular direction. It looked to me like he was hunting and looking around for some signs. After I had been walking for fifteen or twenty minutes, I got a glimpse of him up in front of me. I moved as close as I could, always keeping a tree between the hunter and myself. Finally I came to a place where the trees were too thin for cover, so I figured I might as well walk up to him and check him out. Since the snow was light and really fluffy, I could walk without making any noise.

When I had covered about half the ground between the hunter and myself, all of a sudden he dropped down on one knee and spun around shooting a semi-automatic 22 rifle in a full circle!! He spun right across me from left to right firing all the time. I was so mad and scared I wanted to ring his crazy neck!! From the look on his face, he was one scared hunter, too. He just dropped his gun in the snow after he realized where he had shot and what could have happened. He had figured he was the only person in the woods for miles. I always figure when I get to heaven I'll find my guardian angel with a couple .22 bullet holes in him.

I Should Have Driven

One night there were these two officers working together. The passenger sits in what is called the jump seat. This means, if a car is stopped, the passenger has to bail out as fast as he can and get to the vehicle being stopped before the occupants of the vehicle can bail out and run. You have to be fast, and there is not much time for thinking.

On this night a car was spotted shining, so our two officers came up behind it without any lights on. They then followed it for a ways to see what they were doing. After awhile they figured they may as well stop them and check them out for a firearm. From a pitch dark patrol car, suddenly there were lights everywhere, headlights, both spotlights, and a blue overhead light on. Both vehicles rolled down the road a couple hundred yards before they came to a complete stop on the very edge of the gravel road.

The officer, the one in the passenger seat that does not have time to think, is off and running for the vehicle being stopped before the driver can get the patrol unit stopped and into park. As the driver finally gets up to the vehicle that had been shining, he sees that it is an old couple and there is nothing in the car. They are just lookers. He thanks them and all of a sudden realizes his partner has never made it to the suspect's vehicle.

Our driver goes back to the patrol car and starts to back up to find out what happened to the officer that had bailed out of the passenger side door. By the way, when he bailed out so fast, he left the door open (passenger side), and it stayed that way. As our driver backed up a couple hundred yards, all of a sudden he heard "whamp" as something hit the still open door!

The driver jumped out of the patrol car and ran around to the passenger side in time to see what was left of his buddy climbing up out of a deep ditch right next to the edge of the road. He was a sight to see.

It seems that as the patrol unit was stopping he swung open the door and leaped out around it to get up to the suspected poacher's car as fast as he could. The only problem was that as he went around the door, he came to a startling conclusion. There was no longer anything under his feet, and he was falling through the air into about a ten foot deep ditch! All this time the driver of the patrol unit was pulling the rest of the way up behind the vehicle they were stopping figuring his buddy was already there. NO, he was half dead laying back in a ditch. Finally he got up and started to climb the ten feet up out of the ditch, wet, sore, and hurt. He just cleared the edge of the ditch and stepped onto the road when his buddy in the patrol car (with the passenger side door open) came flying backward looking for him! You guessed it. "Whamp!" The open door picks him off and throws him back into the ditch for the second time. He was sore, but he lived. However, he did tell me it was not one of his better nights. On the other hand, his buddy was scared to death, because when he heard that "Whamp", he thought he had run him over!

Chapter 9
My Hunting Buddies

For years, since my boys have grown up and moved away, I have been taking youth out hunting with me. Some of these are those whose dad cannot get time to take them, or they may not have a man that lives at home to take them out. It provides for some real interesting times and some real mind enlightening sayings. For years I have had this saying that I tell the youth I work with, "A teenager thinking can be a dangerous thing to behold." The other saying that I use over and over with youth that I wholeheartily believe is, "Learning to work hard will overcome a multitude of shortcomings." I like doing things with youth, and here are a couple of stories about taking them out hunting.

Boy First, Dad Later

Up in Schoolcraft County, in Michigan's U.P., we do a lot of jump shooting for waterfowl. This means that you and your hunting buddies try to sneak up on a lake or pond, jump the ducks, and shoot at them as they fly away. There are around four hundred lakes, plus rivers and ponds, throughout the county, so you never run out of places to hunt. The best part of it is that most of the time you can hunt all day without running into another hunter. Weekends are usually the busy days.

This one day a hunting buddy and myself were jump shooting some beaver ponds. We had shot a few ducks and made plans to check out this long wide pond. Seeing that my hunting buddy is a lot better shot than me (I have problems with ducks that are dead and don't know it, so they fly away), I put him down on the near end of the lake and told him I would sneak down to the far end and put the ducks up for him.

It was one of those days that started out cold, so you dressed warm enough to sit over decoys the first couple hours. Later in the day when the sun comes out, it gets real warm. It was a long trip down to the far end of the lake, but I had spotted some ducks down there so it would not all be in vain, I hoped. I sneaked around and through the brush and started to sweat like crazy in all my gear. I looked out and saw this flock of mallards swimming away from shore, so I knew they had spotted me. I didn't care since I was the scarer today just trying to put them up over my hunting buddy. Crawling along carrying a shotgun, I was really sweating now, but I was almost there. All of a sudden the whole flock took off, circled out on the lake, and just like we planned, flew down to the far end where my then best buddy was hidden while waiting on them. The ducks set their wings and went right in on him. I waited til they hit the water, I waited as they swam, in fact I waited till they took off again and left the pond!!! No shots were ever fired down on the end where my buddy was supposed to be.

I started back down the edge of the pond and yelled, "Johnny!" a couple of times. Off over the horizon I heard a faint voice from the area where we had parked the truck. I walked back and up the hill to the truck and asked my now ex-buddy, "Where in the world were you? The ducks landed right where you were SUPPOSED to be!" He looked at me with all seriousness and said, "I got hungry, so I came back to the truck for an apple." "An apple?! You mean, I sweated and crawled along a marsh for 3/4 of a mile to put some ducks over you and all this time you were back at the truck eating an apple?!"

Hunting with teenagers could cause serious brain damage to adults!!

But, Then There's Dad

Later, we met some other waterfowl hunters we know, a father and son team. This crew of father and son went off to hunt a dark marsh, getting there well before daylight, so they could be all set up when daylight and shooting hours arrived. Dad went up one side of the lake in the dark while the son went up the other side. This is so that no matter what they spot at daylight they will be in front of someone. As luck would have it, the geese all took off and left the lake for the grain fields before daylight. But hold it!! As daylight comes and shooting hours arrive, there is a nice flock of ducks on the lake. They are right over there swimming on Dad's side of the lake. The son waits, and waits, and waits, but no Dad shooting at them or scaring them up so they will fly over his way. They are too far out of range for him to shoot at. After all is lost and the ducks took off to follow the geese to the grain fields, the boy took off looking for Dad. Could he have been hurt? Did he have a heart attack?

Could it be nothing?! He finds dad sleeping in the cab of the pickup. Since he had been cold and tired sitting out there before daylight, he just went back and fell asleep. I guess we cannot blame it all on teenagers after all.

Another Teenager

There was this other teenage boy whose dad was a school teacher so could not get out early in the morning to take him goose hunting. (Now, we could go out before school, set our decoys, and have our geese and be back to town for the boys to get to school.) So, I told this boy we would pick him up and take him hunting with us.

Now you may laugh at some of my stories, but I do take my hunting seriously. I like to have fun and goof off, but I don't do it while out hunting. It just sometimes happens that way. All that this boy had was a 20 gauge single shot shotgun, so I gave him one of my 12 gauge semi-automatics to use. Besides, you have to use steel shot on waterfowl, and we only had 12 gauge steelshot.

We went out to a grain field before daylight and set up our decoys. I had the newer hunter down the fence row from me and my usual hunting buddy was out across the field. Sure enough, as shooting hours came so did the geese off Big Bay De Noc on Lake Michigan. They came over the trees, circled the field, dropped down, and set their wings to come into the decoys. At just the right time, I pulled up and shot and got my two geese to fill my limit. The teenager next to me fired once, got a goose, but did not fire again. I did not think much of it. Across the field the third member of our party got his two geese as they took off. A little later a flock of geese came in and our new hunter filled his limit, so it was off in a rush to get back to town and in school on time.

The next day it was the same way. Off before daylight, set up the decoys, wait on the geese. Here they come over the trees into the decoys. We shoot. I get my two, buddy number one gets his two, and our new hunting buddy fires only once and gets one. We all meet at the corner of the fence, and I asked the one boy, who only fires one shot at a time with a three shot semi-automatic shotgun, "Why are you only firing one time when you can get two geese?" His buddy speaks up and says, "He's trying to figure out how the empty casing comes out so fast and where it goes!" I said, "Your kidding me, right?" But they were not! It seems that this youth had never fired a semi-automatic shotgun before and could not figure out how a shell could get out of the gun and a new one into the chamber without you seeing it. I had to tell him, "Don't figure it out! Just shoot. We don't have to know why it works, just so it works!" Now two or three years later, he is an excellent shot and really likes his waterfowl hunting.

Food for thought: One day I was riding around with my hunting buddy. In the Cooks area of Schoolcraft County, there is a big microwave tower. As we were driving along, he looked at me and said with all seriousness, "Mr. Walker, is that where my mom gets the power for her microwave oven?" I gave him one of those looks that lets a teenager know he blew it. At the same time I was thinking, "I never thought of that."

To Live Is To Learn

One day we were out hunting for waterfowl. But, we carried our bows in the vehicle in case we wanted to sit a couple of hours at evening for deer. On this day we had my little red truck and were going down a gravel road. All of a sudden I stopped, and right back behind us stood a great big deer broad side, a perfect shot. My buddy slipped out of the truck, got his bow out of the back, unzipped the case, and took the bow out and put an arrow on the string. He took a couple steps toward the deer that just stood there, pulled back, aimed and let go! A perfect shot right in the middle of a jackpine tree!! (Did you ever try to get a broad-head hunting arrow out of a tree? What a project!)

It seems that (on day two of bow hunting) everything was going fine. We had spotted this nice big deer not too far away. He had gotten out, sneaked around the truck to get his bow out, and got it ready. He had taken a couple steps for a perfect shot, pulled back, aimed his arrow, released the string and at the same instance remembered yesterday!! You see, yesterday he had spotted a deer, got his arrow ready, pulled back and shot at it. All of a sudden, he felt like his arm was on fire!!! He had forgotten to put his forearm protection on before he shot, and he bruised his arm like you wouldn't believe. Being an average teenager, he may learn slowly, but he learns. The fiery pain from the day before all came back to him, so he moved his arm at the last second just as he released the string to keep from hitting it again. Therefore, he got a tree instead of a deer.

Food for thought: Did you ever stop and think about all the people that say, "I got my deer last night." when they really mean they got it last evening (before dark). It's just a phrase that can get you teased. My hunting buddy finally got a deer big enough that he could not eat it all at one sitting. He came over as proud as could be. He told me that he was about ready to leave his blind, in fact he was putting his gear away and making noise. He looked up and saw this buck and shot it "last night". I sure like to give teenagers a hard time and tease them, so I just had to come up with this little jingle for him that I keep singing for him all the time. "Star light, star bright, please help me get a deer tonight."

O' To Be Young Again

Seeing that my boys are grown up and gone, I try to find someone to take hunting that does not have an opportunity. There are a couple of boys under ten that I take with me quite often. Their dad is a farmer and cannot get out during harvest time in the fall, so they enjoy going off with me. The only thing is, when you hunt with youth you tend to discover how old you really are. Here are a few things that may help you find out what age hunting group you are now a part of.

1- You take a couple of six or seven year old boys out duck hunting with you. As you lay in the fence row watching the decoys waiting for something to come in, one of the boys says, "There's some ducks over there!!" There are?? You mean over that way? OK, if you say so. You look but since you see nothing but the specks on your bifocals, you tell them, "Keep your head down, or you'll scare them off." (Just til they get into an old man's range of eyesight.)

2- You keep moving your apples at your deer blind closer so you can see them better. Now you have one real advantage, for you can reach out and get an apple to eat without ever leaving your blind.

3- Somehow the trip into your deer blind gets longer and longer and the bait bucket (the same 5-gallon bucket) gets heavier and heavier each year. The step you take to get into your blind gets higher and tougher to make each year, too.

4- You have to take that little gadget from your wife's sewing room to get your fishing line through the eyes of your hook.

5- You get halfway through the three steps in loading your muzzle loader and forget which step you're on.

6- Either the stock on your gun has grown, or the iron sights have moved farther out on the barrel.

7- You step into a chuckhole while hunting or fishing, and now your whole boot gets full of water instead of your being able to jump back out quick enough that only your sock gets wet.

8- Your wife is getting so old that she cannot remember where you put your hunting gear from the year before.

9- Your seven year old hunting buddy offers to carry your gear so you will not get so tired.

10-The hills to that old favorite hunting or fishing spot have gotten higher, the mud holes have gotten deeper, and the slippery spots really surprise you now.

11-Instead of taking candy bars or apples to your deer blind, you now take Maalox and prunes.

12-For the hundreth time the day before going hunting, you are told, "If you should get anything, make sure you get someone to help you get it out. Don't try to do it yourself!" And you're going rabbit hunting.

13-Your 4-wheeler has a handicap permit, so you can park at your deer blind.

14-Your kids start buying you those funny Christmas gifts meant for old people with which they cannot hurt themselves.

15-And last, your wife tells you, "You may as well go hunting, for you never get anything done around the house anymore." Plus, she is pretty sure your days of bringing something home are over.

But, look at the good side. There are always those out there trying to keep up with the youth that are still a lot younger than you are. Someday they will be in your shoes-then where will you be?

Chapter 10
Fish Reports

(These usually have little or nothing to do with fishing.) I get asked all the time when selling my book, "Just what is a Fish Report?"For all the years I have been writing the "Fish Report" for the Manistique Pioneer-Tribune, I have yet to figure out just what it really is. I guess the best way to describe it is to say it's a "Whatever-Happens-to-Cross-My-Mind-Real-Early-Tuesday-Morning-When-I-Sit-to-Type-Up-a-Fish Report". It started out being a weekly fishing information column, but then I started telling the readers about what took place during the week and it became a story-telling article. With all the questions I have been asked, I decided to include a few actual "Fish Reports" in this chapter. Understand that these four are just to give you an idea of what has been in a fish report because there have been fish reports on things that happened while someone was hunting in Canada and Pennsylvania, plus a story on frogging in Missouri. Always remember that everyone likes to tell a Game Warden their favorite story, so I just learned to listen to them all.

Now, some "Fish Reports" are serious, some are humorous, some are just stories.

Fish Report: #-1 1-4-94

Well, we are into the new year and there is no doubt that winter is upon us. It sure was pretty out the other day with the big snow- flakes and the weather being a little warmer. I got the snowmachine out, and my daughter and I went for a ride up the Haywire Grade. With all the snow on the trees, it sure was an enjoyable trip.

They are getting a few fish out on Indian Lake, but they are not setting any records. Needless to say, be careful out on the ice.

I want to take a couple minutes and say something about what I saw on TV the other night. I also read about it in the newspapers. Sometimes we don't really stop and take the time to think about people involved in things. We know they are there, we realize what they do, but unless we are involved, we kind of brush it off.

The other night on TV, I saw a group of people sitting around talking to the TV crew (that maybe are not too bright). There was a Conservation Officer, a State Trooper, a sheriff deputy, some people from Search and Rescue Team, and others.

Now, I know for a fact (Because they live in our town of Manistique) that most of those on TV being interviewed have a family, a spouse, maybe some kids back home. YET!! The night before when a call came in after dark about a party who had gone through the ice on a snowmo- bile, off they went. Out on the same lake, on the same bad ice to try to save a life. Deep down, having been there, you know that your efforts to find the party alive are pretty slim. Do you stop and think about the spouse and kids back home? Not really, because you have a job to do. If you happen to go through the ice and drown too, will anyone really care besides the family? Maybe and maybe not. In fact, there would be those that would say how dumb it was to go out there after one snowmachine already went through. Do you have a plan and a method in your rescue attempt? Yes, but even then there is always a good chance that someone else may get hurt. How do I know that these people, whose whole goal is to help someone else, never really stop and think about the price their family may pay? I have been there.

A couple of years back, I was riding in a State Police car with the

Lieutenant from the Post. A call came on the radio that a lady had observed a snowmobile go through the ice and there was a party laying on the ice out in the middle of Indian Lake. This snowmobiler-fisherman had cut across the lake trying to get those nice big fish that always bite when the ice is getting bad. On his way back across the lake, his snowmobile went through, and so did he. In fact, when he got back on top of the ice he went through again. The Lt. and I drove over to the lady's house, and she pointed the party out to us. About this time, a sheriff's deputy came up. As the Lieutenant tried to get more help on the radio, the sheriff's deputy and I took a metal boat and pushed it out on the lake. We each got on the side and worked our way out to the man laying on the ice in the middle of the lake. The fisherman grabbed the back of the boat, and we then turned the boat around to head back for shore. As we were doing this, the deputy went through the ice, but he held onto the side of the boat and pulled himself back up. The three of us made it back to shore without anyone getting hurt.

One other time I was called out to Lake Michigan, south of Gulliver, where the undertow had pulled a boy under. A crew from the Gulliver Fire Department was there trying to find the youth as members of his family watched and hoped for a miracle. Three-four firemen holding onto a rope were out in these big waves hoping to feel the boy and pull him in. All of a sudden, as we all stood there helpless, the rope broke and these three-four firemen were being batted around in the waves. I thought for sure that there would be a couple more people drowned that day because the water was so rough. By the grace of God, they all got back to shore.

What am I trying to say? Thank goodness there are those around, like the crew on TV the other night, that never really stop and think of the price their family may pay for their actions. Instead, when there is a call and a need they go off, not thinking of themselves, but hoping, just maybe, this one will end like 911 on TV, and they will get there in time to save a life, not recover a victim. My hat goes off to the Sheriff's Deputy, Conservation Officers, State Troopers, the Search and Rescue crew, fire departments, and all the others from our little town that help out. When you see them, let them know you now realize what they do and tell them thanks because you never know who may need them next.

Fish Report: #-2 7-27-93

Well, summer weather sure has been nice for the last week or so! It sure seems to bring the people out, and the boardwalk is getting its share of use. I guess a person has to say that we have been pretty lucky with our weather up here. We get a snowstorm, but big deal. We expect to have them. We get some heavy rains if things go right, and it will run off into Lake Michigan. If Lake Michigan ever gets full, then we may really have a problem. All in all things have been pretty good up our way.

With the little break in the weather, fishing improved a little in our area. It really is something the way a week of warm weather can change the water levels and improve fishing. They got a few brook trout and some nice bass on the lakes and creeks up north. They were also getting a few nice pike.

There was a dad I talked to the other day that had been camping out at Indian Lake with his kids, and the wife got to go, too. He was talking about the great time they had. They bought a camper trailer and fixed it up to hopefully keep the rain on the outside where it belonged. Their kids are grade school age, so they spent a week camping with them. It sure got me thinking.

Do you realize how many times a father, whose sons have grown up and left, gets to walking someplace and all of a sudden he feels that something is missing or just different than it was before? Then, he gets to thinking back years before when this walk in the morning, or it could be anytime of the day, was a special walk he took with his boys. Maybe just to talk, or maybe just to get a pop or something to eat, but just a nothing time together, just Dad and the kids. Back then you never thought too much of it. The kids were little and in grade school, and it would be years before they grew up and went off on their own. There were a couple million things that you wanted to talk to them about and teach them before they grew up, but you had a lot of time yet. So, you spent those fun years with the kids and family doing the little things that make a family special-scaring the fire out of Mom by hiding in the dark and jumping out as she walked by or firing bottle rockets under the door when Mom went to the only place where she thought she would be safe from those boys. All of a sudden you look around, and those grade school kids are not grade-schoolers anymore. They now have a driver's license and are talking about college, but you are lucky enough to still have those walks and good times together. You listen to their plans and are so proud of them. A few years are still left before they graduate from high school, so you still have time to enjoy them. Then all of a sudden, your grade schooler that became a high schooler is off to college. However, there are still those summers and college breaks for your walks and talks, and the kids have grown up so much. Then something comes along that makes you realize that those walks and talks are going to be history. She is about 5'3" or so, blonde hair, eyes that look only at him, and you realize that someone else is going to be taking those walks with him. You wouldn't have it any other way, but how could it happen so fast? It's supposed to take years to go from that grade school kid out camping with Mom and Dad til they're off on their own. That many years could not have flown by so quickly, but the dreams and memories are still there, and once or twice a year, just maybe, you will be able to get together and take those little walks again. Only, now they will mean even more because you know how important they are and how fast the years go by and things change.

Mom and Dad, don't let the years slip by. Enjoy the kids and the good times while they are here.

Fish Report: #-3 10-13-92

Well, if you stepped outside already this morning, you can sure feel that bite in the air. It's getting about that time to get the long handles out ! The only problem is, you put them on in the morning to sit in a duck blind over some decoys and it feels great to be nice and warm, but as the day warms up and the frost burns off, you decide to take a walk into a beaver pond to see if there are any ducks on it. Now it is up in the fifties and as you do a slow melt-down, you wonder if it was such a good idea to wear those long handles after all.

The leaves have really fallen the last couple of days with the winds we have had. Also, a lot of the geese have left to let those hunters south of us get a chance at them. The duck hunting is so-so with a few around, but nothing to brag about. The pats are still trying to prove they should be on the endangered species list. Before the cold snap they were having a lot of fun after woodcock.

But it has really been a pretty fall to be out there just enjoying things. In fact, I told somebody the other day that I have already forgotten how bad summer was because the last month has been so nice. I took a big chance yesterday and put up the lawn mover, put on some storm windows, and picked up things around the yard just in case. There were a few of those white objects flying around in the air yesterday as I was duck hunting.

I guess I will take a few lines to tell you about how down a hunter can get. I happened to turn on my TV the other day and came across an outdoor show. I should have skipped over it quickly because it was from downstate, but on this show, they had one of those so-called deer hunting exspurts with about a hundred years of college. Here sits this guy, dressed like he just fell out of a Ted Williams book, telling everything that will not work if you are after whitetail deer. Step by step he covers just about everything I do having fun getting ready for deer season trying to outwit that nice buck. In fifteen minutes he destroyed my whole hunting program! Here this guy (the exspurt) sits on TV telling the whole world, at least in Michigan, what not to do, and here sits a dad that loves to get out of doors and who with his boys has shot over thirty deer using the methods that "will not work"!! Now what am I going to do?!! Then I recall what a certain spud farmer out at Cooks told me one day as we talked about these so called exspurts. His definition of an exspurt was, "A drip under pressure." So, seeing my non-working methods work and I have fun having fun, I guess I will just keep on using them.

The other day someone that knows I like to hunt came up to me and told me about this new- to-me duck hunting pond. He said, "Go down to the T intersection and take a left. Go down across the creek til you come to the first road to the right by a big bunch of birch trees. Only don't look for the birchtrees, for they cut them a few years back. Go down this road thru the pines til you come to the end, then turn around. Come back til you find the place where there is a truck turn-a-round. Park here and walk through the pines, down over the hill, through the marsh til you come to the duck pond. We did all this, and as the dog was getting the two ducks we shot, I looked around. All of a sudden I told my hunting partner, "Look, over there across the pond is where we ate lunch last Saturday!!" We drove and sweated getting to the other side of a pond we had been driving to for years! Oh well, the two ducks made it worth it.

Fish Report: #-4 6-8-93

Well, if it weren't for all the rain, fishing would be getting better. The cherries are in blossom, and the bugs have really come alive the last few weeks. Both of these are signs that the fish should start biting. Fishermen are getting a few pike and a few nice pan fish up north. They are also getting a few nice walleye.

You want to watch for deer as you drive around. It seems that there are a lot of them being hit by cars in the last month. With these plastic cars it, does not take much to do a lot of damage.

The final say on this fall's hunting seasons should be acted on this month by the DNR Commission. After this we should know what changes we are in for. Eino has one for them to think about. One of the rules they are trying to get passed is that any deer blind made of other than "natural" stuff must be removed from the woods each night. Now if you look at this in a fair and impartial way, you have to remember that wood comes from trees, trees come from the woods, so any wood used is just being taken back to its roots and placed back in its environment. Right? Then, you have to remember that plastic is a by-product of oil, oil comes from decomposed trees and such, so if you have any plastic, this, too, is just being put back where it started from. Right? So remember, it's important to understand what "natural" materials are.

After much deep study, I have come to the conclusion that fishermen are nuts! The other day we were driving along, and it was raining like crazy. Out in the lake sits a number of boats with "fishermen" trying to catch fish. It is cold, the wind is blowing, it is raining cats and dogs, and someone is trying to catch a fish. Well, look at it this way. It was too wet to cut the grass, so why not go fishing?

Then, there were a couple guys that went fishing one day. They took along one of the guy's little brother who is not little anymore and is a teenager now. They have this secret fishing spot that only they know about. Right, tell me another one. So to keep it a secret (and brotherly love being what it is), they blindfold "little" brother to take him into their secret fishing lake. I think the reason they did not want "little" brother to know about their secret lake is because he is a better fisherman than they are and may return and catch the fish they hope to catch!

Someday a person is going to have to do a study to see what costs more per pound, the game we get when hunting or the fish we catch while fishing. Per pound, I am not sure if either one is a real smart investment.

Question: Did you ever see one of these fishing programs on TV where they spend all day catching 3-4 inch pan fish? Then, the man throws his pole in the bottom of the boat and says how great it's been? In fact, I have to wonder sometimes if there are any undersized fish in the lakes they fish in. They always go fishing with a TV star or a sports star, but did you ever think about their poor kids sitting home wondering why Dad never takes them out fishing? Maybe I missed the show that shows Dad spending all afternoon in his new $20,000 bass boat, baiting worms for his kids, trying to unmess the lines when the kids all try to cast out at the same time, getting a hook out of Johnny's ear, and just having normal-family-type fun while out fishing on a weekend afternoon-or, after all this "fun", trying to explain to the game warden how they are one life jacket short. The kids were all wearing them around the house while Dad was loading the boat, and one must have left his home when he used the bathroom. Sometimes I think these shows tend to distort the real fun of fishing.

As you sit and think about the weather, here's food for thought. Two more weeks and we have our longest day of the year, then we are heading back toward winter.

O'well, remember Fathers Day and take Dad out fishing.

Grandpa Theiler

Dad at camp

Grandpa Walker and Dad
November 1949

Chapter 11
My Dad, My Hero

Well, did you ever do something without thinking about it? It was just a reaction? Then you stop and realize that your dad always did it the same way. You then start thinking about all the little habits you picked up from your parents. This chapter is about mine and how lucky I was.

In my newspaper column, I have written a number of times about that lump a lot of us U.P. boys get in our throat when November 15th rolls around each year. My dad has been gone for around twenty-five years now, but when November comes and the first snow arrives, firearm deer season cannot be far away. When this time of year used to come, God had to have made it for U.P. boys and their dads! There were great times had throughout the year, but firearm deer season was just that special time for us. It meant getting to go to camp (maybe even miss a couple of days of school if your grades were up) and spend some time with Dad and his brother, plus some friends from downstate. Life was great back then. In fact, even after I started with the Michigan Conservation Department, I still got to spend a couple days around the first of deer season with Dad. Back then, if you are old enough to remember, the firearm deer season started a couple days earlier in the U.P. than it did downstate. So, I got to rush up to camp, get to be with Dad and my brothers who were still in high school, and rush back down-state to work the opening of deer season down there. Even now after all these years, that lump is still there when I think about my Dad and how he made life special for us. Come November 15th each year I still miss him.

Dad, Wisdom

My dad quit school to go to work with his dad on a train out at a lumber camp. He never finished high school, but as I think back, he sure had a lot of wisdom when it came to us boys. I guess it goes to show that wisdom does not come from books. Knowledge does, but anyone that wants to learn can have wisdom in everyday family matters, just like my dad did.

I think back to those times in the 50's that Dad would take me out hunting and out to camp. The two of us usually went together, for my three brothers are quite a bit younger than I am. So, it was dad and me back then. I have to laugh at how he must have felt as we poked along in his "Bug". (This was a Model-T made into a hunting vehicle. Nobody heard of a 4x4 pickup back then.) We would go up to the relatives' farm on the Norwich Road near Ontonagon and get ready to go hunting. We would have to pump up all four tires with a hand pump because they never held air except for the two months of hunting season. Dad would set the spark lever, get the crank out, and go around front to start the "Bug". It always started, and off we would go, chains banging on the homemade wooden fenders, no protection but a windshield, Dad and his boy off for a day in the woods. Getting back to Dad, I could not tell you how many times we would see a pat along one of the old railroad grades, and Dad would tell me, "Get out. Slow, slow.... get your gun out... Keep an eye on the birds. Hurry now, they're getting spooky.... Watch where you point your gun... Too late! They're gone." Dad never got mad and never jumped out to shoot because I was too slow or too excited that even if I got the gun out and loaded I missed umpteen pats before I ever got one. But, the day I got my first one, was dad ever excited and was I proud!

There sure was a lesson learned during this time with dad and it was that not everything works out the first time a person tries it. You may have to just step back, take a deep breath, and try again. But if you have someone there helping and encouraging you, it sure is great when you finally make it. I think back as to how lucky I was to have Dad and Mom in my early years, then later my wonderful wife and kids. Life sure would have been empty without them.

One of the other things I think is really important that I learned from Dad was this. During our hours and hours together, whether it was walking while hunting or at camp, Dad would talk to me about life in general.

He would teach me about how a man should behave, what was expected of a man and a father, and how you should react to things. Some of these things were to correct me for things I had goofed up on while growing up, but with Dad, while out at camp, it was not too heavy on me. Being at camp with a dad you knew loved you, when you were corrected about something, it did not seem like you were being bawled out. It was just your hunting buddy teaching you something for later in life. I still marvel at the wisdom my dad had doing things this way.

The second lesson I learned was that in the right place at the right time you can talk to almost any teenager about things, and they will listen to you. Just ask some of the youth I used to take hunting with me, (years later) how often I talked to them about school work, their plans for life, and the rights and wrongs of growing up. Do they listen? Maybe like I did with my dad, but they are always ready to go out hunting the next time just like I was with my dad. Plus, they know that there is at least one person that cares about them and how they will turn out.

Another thing that comes to mind while thinking back is the fact that I got to learn about my dad. I got to see him in action, not only telling me things, but doing them. Back in the 50's we used to always get our five birds each, almost ever day we went out. After we got the fifth one, our guns were put away! It did not matter how many we might see on the way home, they were for another day. We had our limit. If it was deer season and my dad saw a nice buck, he never shot it and asked us boys to put our tag on it. He would sit and let it go by and hope it would make its way by one of us. They never did and how mad we would get at Dad when we found out he let a buck walk by him hoping one of his boys would get it. But, what a father-son partnership was built up.

The lesson I learned here was that my dad was honest even when nobody was watching and nobody would have said anything if he had acted different. I think one of the greatest compliments a person can be paid is when someone says, "I may not agree with the way they do things, but one thing you can say for them, they're honest." I can remember the day I asked my Dad a question (You see, it was common knowledge during the "big depression" that a lot of families had to use government beef to make ends meet. Then, at school a teenage boy would always hear about those that never got out of the habit and had been out hunting the night before.) "Dad, how come you never shoot an illegal deer or violate?" (This is a teenage boy asking.) Dad told me, "Son, how in the world could I tell you kids how important doing your school work and getting good grades are on your own, without cheating, if I was bringing home illegal game? Would what I told you and the things I asked of you have any meaning?" (I'm not sure you are supposed to answer a question with a question, but it sure was food for thought.)

How many men I could tell you about that worked hard, would never steal or cheat a person, but they never paid any attention to fish and game laws. Years later, their kids came along and never drew the lines the same place dad did. They not only shot a few deer out of season, but broke into hunting camps, stole anything that wasn't tied down, and Dad footed the bills and could never understand why. Why? A double standard does not work. Dad felt you couldn't tell your kids one thing and you, yourself, do another.

I'll close this chapter by saying, that for as long as my Mom and Dad were alive, if I was buying a home or a car, I would call them and ask their opinion. They never really told me what to do or what not to do, but if they had observed some hidden danger that they had learned already, they would have let me know or at least warned me about it. Now years later, my two married sons will call Mom and Dad to ask their advice on some things. Some things are way over our heads in this day and age, but it sure is a good feeling to know they trust and think enough of their parents to call and ask. Maybe what I learned from my parents is still working in this computer generation.

I just hope that you young people that read this book will stop long enough to enjoy the time spent at camp with Dad and Grandpa. The day will come that you will head out to camp with nothing but memories. Your kids have come and gone, grown up, as time continues to fly by. It seemed like I only blinked, and they rode off for a life of their own. Maybe once in awhile getting a few days off to make it to camp with Dad, but not too often, for they now have a life and family of their own to take care of. You will sit in a rocking chair that your dad before you sat in wondering where all the years went so fast. Then, as you close your eyes, you can see Dad sitting there as you hunt deer mice with your Red Ryder BB gun.... So many years back- or was it just yesterday that you and Dad were here? Parents, take your kids hunting and fishing. Don't raise them in front of a TV or those video games they stare at for hours on end!

For years I had a license plate on the front of my car that read; "Take your kids hunting, instead of hunting for your kids". How true this can be.

Chapter 12
Snowmobiling

Well, snowmobiling is an interesting sport. Back in the 70's it was big, I mean real big! But then for a few years it kind of went downhill with fewer and fewer snowmachines. In the last few years it has really mushroomed again. It must be those rich farmers from outside the U.P. that can afford to buy those expensive snowmachines and all the equipment that goes with them.

But if you have ever spent any time on a snowmachine, you will have tales to tell. In this section you will read about a few of mine. I have to wonder, as the years go by and the pains of old age creep up on me, how many of them are the result of all the miles I rode on a snowmachine? I know a few of my gray hairs came from some of my snowmobile trips. Over the years I always figured if I had ridden my snowmachines in a straight line I could have really gone somewhere instead of around in circles. There were at least three or four snowmachines I saw arrive new and leave worn out by all the miles put on them. Here are a few snowmobiling adventures.

Oops!

On this particular day I was out on a snowmobile patrol working with another officer. We had been working in the deer yards and checking the snowmobile trails. We went up the Haywire Grade going north out of Manistique, then cut across to hit the Jungle Trail coming into the Big Springs deer yard. Since it was after dark when we arrived at the deer yard, we spent a little time there checking out the traffic using the plowed logging roads into the areas where cedar was being cut. We left the deer yard and came south and hit M-149 near Big Springs. We then headed towards the west shore of Indian Lake. The officer I was working with on this day lived on M-149, so when we came to the area of the state park, he headed off toward home. I went into the park to hit the lake and cut across it for home.

It was completely dark by this time, and the wind had started to blow hard as snow was now falling heavy. I hit Indian Lake off the access site at the Westshore State Park. As I started across the lake holding to a southerly direction, I could not make out the far side of the lake through all the blowing snow. I kept going and about the time I must have been about halfway across the lake, the headlight on my snowmobile blew out ! There I sat out in the middle of Indian Lake without any headlights, all by myself now, and without even a flashlight. The snow let up a little, and I saw what I figured was a Mercury yard light on the south end of the lake. I started off heading my snowmachine right for the light that kept fading in and out of my sight with the blowing snow. Slowly, I came getting closer and closer to the yard light until I could just make it out. All of a sudden, my snowmachine jumped up over something, launched over a drift, and dropped down, then stopped!

I had found my light ! Here I sat, about four feet from a plate glass sliding door, looking right into someone's family room at the fire burning in the fireplace! I was sitting on their patio deck ! Thank goodness I was not going too fast, or I would have landed right in their family room through the plate glass doors. It wasn't a Mercury yard light after all.

As quickly and as quietly as I could, I got off my snowmachine, picked up the back, and went back out onto the lake. Then I followed the shoreline down to a road and headed for home. I often wondered what the owner of the house I landed at thought when he observed those snowmobile tracks on his deck the next day? Well, now he knows.

'Tis Not Good

I had just been issued a brand new 440 snowmachine that was really a nice machine. Now, you have to read all the stories in this book and understand what Conservation Officers started out with for snowmachines to understand how we felt when we were issued a new one like this. Somehow going from an 8-horsepower, single banger, to a 440 that rides like a car and really flies was quite a deal. Here I was checking it over in my yard and ready to take a ride up north. I could leave my house, hit the pipeline, then go over and hit the Haywire Grade snowmobile trail and ride for as long as I wanted.

What a deal! The machine was free to me, the gas and oil for it was supplied, and I got paid for doing what other people had to either take a vacation for or cram into a weekend. What more could a guy ask for?

I worked my way up north that day, first checking some fishermen on Island Slough on the Manistique River, then checking a few deer yards. I got about thirty miles up north and decided to turn around and head back toward home because it was getting dark. I headed back down the groomed snowmobile trail just enjoying the scenery and having a great time riding my new machine. When I came to an area where the old railroad grade was real straight and as smooth as could be, I decided to see what this 440 snowmobile would do. I got it going pretty good and was totally impressed and having myself a ball when all of a sudden, my new snowmachine decided to coast to a stop! Just like it was out of gas! It could not be seeing I had filled it up just before I left the house, but I checked it anyway. Sure enough, I had plenty of gas.

I checked the plug wires using my flashlight because now it was dark (I learned to carry a flashlight after all that happened in the OOPS story). I looked around making sure everything was attached and could not find anything wrong. I turned it over a couple of times, but it just sputtered and would not fire. I finally decided to take the spark plugs out and see if they were getting gas. Using the light from my flashlight, I pulled both plugs and laid them on the cylinder heads. I then shined my flashlight down the sparkplug holes and thought, "They must make these new snowmachines different from the older ones," for I could see the roller bearings down the sparkplug holes. Now, I knew when I saw bearings down a plug holes that I was in for a long walk home. I looked at the plugs themselves and saw that they were pounded full of aluminum. My dream machine had died on me. My long, dark walk home sure was no dream.

Not Again

A few years back, I found a really good deal on a used snowmachine. It was a 440 that had been driven by a little old lady back and forth from the store. Really, it was-almost. The people that owned it lived on an island and used it to get to the mainland during the winter when the lake froze over. I know a great deal when I see one, and it was love at first sight. So I bought it because I had never owned a snowmachine like this for my own. Besides I did not want my girls, the only kids left home now, to have a deprived childhood without a snowmachine for dad to ride. I loaded it up and brought it home to surprise the wife.

I managed to tell her what a great deal it was and how lucky I was to happen upon it before anyone else. She just stood there with that look in her eye that told me she had heard this same sales pitch on some other items I had bought before. But this was different, it really was a good deal honey! She had to admit that the machine looked great sitting in the driveway on a trailer.

My daughter came home from school, and just to show my wife I had purchased this snowmachine with all the right intentions, I asked her if she wanted to go for a ride with me. Since Cathy was all for it, we got ready and off we went. Now, this had to be more exciting than the above trip because this was my own machine. Even if I did have to buy the gas, who cared? I could take my daughter for a ride on this one; life was great!

We headed up the snowmobile grade to see if we could see some deer in the deer yards. We were just poking along having a great time and enjoying the out of doors. I came to this stretch on the snowmobile trail that was real straight and well groomed, long and smooth. (Going the other direction now from above.) I told Cathy to hang on, and off we went on our new-to-us 440 snowmachine. We came up on the place where the OOPS story took place just cruising along not even thinking of that dumb trip where the state's 440 gave up the ghost. All of a sudden... you guessed it!! It seemed that my own personal dream machine had run out of gas and slowed to a stop ! Now, Mrs. Walker did not raise any dummy, and I wanted to sit on this great looking, no longer running, machine and cry! Only, I couldn't because I had my daughter with me. I knew right away what to do, so I pulled the plugs to see if what I already thought was true; It was. Plugs pounded full of metal, bearings showing in plug holes, and tears in my eyes.

Just look at the bright side I had someone to walk home with in the dark this time. She talked all the way home about how funny it was going to be as Dad tried to explain to Mom what happened to his really great deal on his snowmachine that was only driven by a little old lady back and forth to the store. Sure Dad, tell me another one.

Chapter 13
Kids, You're Special

Well, I have sure received a lot of comments from youth about how they enjoyed my last book, "A Deer Gets Revenge." For that reason, I want to take time in this chapter to talk to them. I guess we all have those times when we do not take time to engage our brains before we do something. I have been guilty of it more than once. I hope all you kids that read this chapter will stop and think a minute about how your parents feel about you. Sometimes in the stress of life they do not always say how they feel, or they may blow it when they really mean to help you out, but you better believe they want you to turn out right. Most important, you should understand that if something were to happen to you there would sure be a big empty spot. As you read my books, you can see how I felt about my dad, but don't you think there would have been the same loneliness for my dad if it had been me and he was the one left with just memories? Please, stop and think before you act. The first story is about my boy, Rob, duck hunting. The second one is out of the Tuscola County paper where I used to work. I have had this article for over twenty years and have used it often even with its gory details to try and get teenagers to think.

Guardian Angels Do Go Hunting

It was during the fall a few years back that a crew of us were going out duck hunting. I had my hunting buddy with me and my dog, Rocky. My boy, Rob, was going with a buddy, and we were to meet later in the day. We both set off to hit some ponds and jump shoot some ducks. It was the last day of season, so we had high hopes.

Johnny and I checked a few lakes and got a couple of ducks when we ran across Robert and Kenny near Mud Lake. We were laughing and talking when Kenny told this story. PS. Don't tell it to the boys' mothers because they never heard it, and things like this are not supposed to happen while you're out to have fun.

Rob and Kenny had checked a couple of lakes and decided to check Frank's Lake near their cabin for ducks. They parked their vehicle and made plans to sneak up on the lake and jump shoot any ducks they spotted there. Their plans worked out just like they were supposed to, and they dropped a couple ducks out in the middle of the lake. Seeing I had the dog and they wanted to check some other lakes, they decided to try and get the ducks without the dog. For some reason, whenever Bob hunted with this crew and they were without a dog, they felt he should replace the dog and retrieve the birds.

My boy went around the lake til he got along the shore as close to the ducks as he could get. He started to wade out into the water to try and reach the ducks. As he worked his way out, all of a sudden he stepped into deep water. This was not the only problem because as he took that step, he found himself stuck in the mud in the bottom of the lake and sinking. The more he tried to get free from the mud the farther down he went in the water. Kenny stood on shore laughing at first, then starting to realize that things were not so funny. All of a sudden all that Kenny could see of Bob was his arm outstretched holding his gun above the water! Kenny started to take off some clothes thinking he may have to try and swim out to help Bob! As he watched, the arm holding the gun out of the water went down out of sight in the water! Now Kenny could see no sign of Bob at all out in the lake. He was about to jump in when all of a sudden, Bob broke the surface of the water and started to swim for shore. These two boys laugh about it now, but they had the scare of their young lives. Kenny really thought that Bob had been done for.

Bob tells us that the mud had such a grip on him that he kept sinking deeper and deeper, and the only thing he could do was go all the way under and try to get his legs free. Thank goodness things worked out. See, Guardian Angels really do go duck hunting with teenagers.

Rudy Petzold had this article in the Tuscola County newspaper years ago and asked, "Pass it on to your own, won't you?"

It came from the office of a Wisconsin Highway Safety Coordinator. It has a sad, quiet, numbing message, but it's true.

I'm Only 17

Agony claws my mind, I am a statistic. When I first got here, I felt very much alone. I was overwhelmed with grief, and I expected to find sympathy.

I found no sympathy. I saw only thousands of others whose bodies were as badly mangled as mine. I was given a number and placed in a category. The category was called "Traffic Fatalities."

The day I died was an ordinary school day. How I wish I had taken the bus! But I was too cool for the bus. I remember how I wheedled the car out of mom. "Special favor", I pleaded. "All the kids drive." When the 2:50 bell rang, I threw my books in the locker. I was free until 8:40 tomorrow morning! I ran to the parking lot--excited at the thought of driving a car and being my own boss, free!

It doesn't matter how the accident happened. I was goofing off-going too fast. Taking crazy chances. But I was enjoying my freedom and having fun.

The last thing I remember was passing an old lady who seemed to be going awfully slow. I heard a deafening crash and felt a terrific jolt. Glass and steel flew everywhere. My whole body seemed to be turning inside out. I heard myself scream.

Suddenly, I awakened. I was very quiet. A police officer was standing over me. Then I saw a doctor. My body was mangled. I was saturated with blood. Pieces of jagged glass were sticking out all over. But, strange that I couldn't feel anything.

Hey!! Don't pull that sheet over my head! I can't be dead! I'm only 17!

I've got a date tonight. I'm supposed to grow up and have a wonderful life. I haven't lived yet. I can't be dead.

Later, I was placed in a drawer. My folks had to identify me. Why did they have to see me like this? Why did I have to look at Mom's eyes when she faced the most terrible ordeal of her life? Dad suddenly looked like an old man. He told the man in charge, "Yes--he is our son."

The funeral was a weird experience. I saw all my relatives and friends walk toward the casket. They passed by, one by one, and looked at me with the saddest eyes I have ever seen. Some of my buddies were crying. A few of the girls touched my hand and sobbed as they walked away.

PLEASE-- SOMEBODY--wake me up!! Get me out of here! I can't bear to see Mom and Dad so broken up. My grandparents are so racked with grief they can barely walk. My brother and sister are like zombies-in a daze. Everybody, no one can believe this. And I can't believe it either.

Please, don't bury me! I'm not dead. I have a lot of living to do. I want to laugh and run again. I want to sing and play. Please don't put me in the ground. I promise if you give me just one more chance, God, I'll be the most careful driver in the whole world. All I want is one more chance. Please, God, I'm only 17!

I know it's pretty graphic, but as you kids read this, stop and think how important you are to Mom and Dad, your grandparents, and those that love you. It would not have to be a traffic accident. It could be a hunting accident or while you're boating. Just a little horseplay and all Dad's dreams will be shattered. Help that guy you call "Dad" to have his dreams come true for you.

Eino and Teivo

Eino and Teivo are two of my favorite people. The next couple of chapters are stories I wrote about the people of Michigan's U.P. Living and growing up in the U.P., you get to see that there is a lot of homespun wisdom up here, wisdom that is not taught in college, but through hard work and hard living. You sit around over a cup of coffee at Plutchak Brothers station in Mass, or at the Crosscut Cafe on M-28, or maybe at Sunny Shores in Manistique, and you get to see and feel what the people of the U.P. are like. The wisdom talked about here would put some of that used in Lansing and Washington to shame. Here sits a guy who just wants to raise his kids to amount to something, have some values, and pay his bills when they are due. When this guy, a native of the U.P. (who thinks Green Bay, Wisconsin, is down South), gives you his word, it is worth something. If he says he will do something for you or pay back what you loaned him, you better believe he will! He is my kind of guy! Before I get into my stories, let me tell you a true one about a U.P. type Eino or Teivo.

A good friend of mine from the Crystal Falls area who now lives in Manistique has this true story told about him. His name is Arvo Kettula. Arvo worked a lot of his life loading railroad ties by hand. He is not a big man, but you better believe he is a strong one after years of throwing railroad ties around. Arvo transferred over to Inland Quarry near Manistique to work on a section crew for the railroad at the quarry. The quarry used trains to move the stones from the pits to the crushers.

For years, Arvo Kettula carried treated railroad ties around as part of his job. Hard work meant nothing to him, because it was a way of life. (Let me say, for you that don't understand what I am going to tell you, I am 6'3" tall and weigh 230 pounds, but as big as I am, I don't think I could lift a treated railroad tie off the ground. Man, they are heavy!) It seems that on this certain day, a new employee of the quarry came along. This new employee was called a Safety Officer, and it was his job to go around and check on working conditions for the workers. Today, he was checking on the section crews laying track in the quarry. As he stood there, along came Arvo with a railroad tie on his shoulder. As Arvo dropped the tie where it was needed, this young safety officer walked up to him. He told Arvo, "You better double up on those ties." Off went

Arvo to do his job, and the Safety Officer stood there checking things out. A short time later, along came Arvo, now with a treated railroad tie on each shoulder!! Not one, but TWO ties!! It seemed that when the young safety officer told Arvo that he had better double up on those ties, to Arvo it could only mean one thing. You were supposed to carry two ties instead of one! This young safety officer actually wanted two men on each tie! Things had never been done that way before. Arvo Kettula is my kind of guy, and he proves that hard work will not kill a good Yooper.

Chapter 14
Yooper Basketball Teams

As I stated in the forward of my first book, basketball was big in the U.P. back when I was a kid. Our town, Ontonagon, had some great teams, and the whole town supported them. If you were in the tournaments, stores would close and just about everybody went to the games. It was a great life, even sitting on the bench watching. At least I got in the games free, and the school bought dinner. Do you realize how few times a boy like myself got to eat out in different towns back in those days? Life was great.

Years later, when I was working down state, I got the chance a number of times to listen to "Down-State" announcers trying to announce a game with a team from the Copper Country. What a laugh we had as they tried to tell who was who from where. Well, this story helps explain it.

Basktball U.P. Style

It is getting toward the end of the basketball season, and there are still a couple U.P. teams making a run at the state championship in their class. Since they have made it through the games held in the U.P. and Northern Lower, now they are going down to the big city to play. I sit here and can still start laughing at the problems they are going to cause, whether it be basketball or any other U.P. sports team playing down state after being in the Copper Country.

The Copper Country, (see Backwoods Glossary) where you have towns with names like: Ontonagon, Winona, Toivola, Osceola, Yondota, Kinnickinnic, Kvidera, Pelkie, and Nisula. The players could also be from Rousseau, Wainola, Monehan, or a dozen other U.P. towns with names from the Motherland, but the towns they are from are not the best part of it!

You have these big time, "Down- State", announcers on the radio or TV used to saying, "Rose, brings the ball down the floor, passes to Weber, over to Smith, back to Jones, to Rose in the corner-he shoots! Off the rim." For them life has been real simple all these years, but that is about to end for the Copper Country teams are on the way! Before we get into the game, let me give you just a few of the names of players on the U.P. teams (found in the Houghton Mining Journal a couple years back). Try a few of these names: Haataja, Kemppianen, Majurin, Verberkmoes, Lamppa, Neimela, Hulkonen, Bertagnoli, Ahola, Ninefeldt, and Gollakner. Then you may have a Jayaramen, Hiltunen, Primeau, Gazvoda, or maybe a Bronczyk, Smigowski, or Yandl all on the same team. If you are lucky you get a few of the more common names from the area thrown in like Maki, Kangas, Aho, and a Haapala.

Couldn't you just picture this on a Saturday afternoon on downstate TV? Haataja born and raised in Yondota is bringing the ball down the floor, he passes over to Kemppianen, cross court to Verbermoes, the ball goes underneath to Jayaramen. It's stolen by Ahola, up court to Smigowski, to Bert Agnoli for a layup! It sure is a lot easier to say, Weber to Rose, underneath to Smith for a layup. Who are from Detroit, Flint, or Grand Rapids, not Toivola, Osceola, or Kvidera.

After looking at the pictures in the local papers of the basketball teams from the Copper Country, the local papers, I think I know now why they do not get those scholarships to them "Big" schools. Now, you have to remember that those guys making millions announcing the games on TV have their "rights", too. Just picture a team of Yoopers making the NCAA Final Four.

First of all, these announcers would not be able to tell the listeners who the players were or where they were from without the aid of an interpreter!! You see, the first group of names are all towns that are or were in the U.P. at one time that had their own little school. Picture this: "Here goes the tip-it's controlled by Verberkmoes over to Majurin, cross court to Haataja, under the basket to Jayaramen again for a layup-he missed! Off the rim, rebounded by Kemppianen from Kinnickinnic, over to Bertagnolia, who brings it down the floor. A screen is set by Gazvoda for Neimela, who shoots, off the rim, Oh! But it's tipped in by Hiltunen, who was born in Osceola, but now lives in Rousseau." Somehow I get the feeling that this should be an Olympic game between two different countries rather than a bunch of kids playing from the Copper Country in the U.P.

I guess we should give some credit to those local U.P. radio stations that have to announce games with these teams year in and year out. Life can get real interesting up here.

Diamond Lumber Crew

Diamond Lumber Bark Crew

Diamond Lumber Blacksmith

Old steam engine log train

Chapter 15
Someone Stole My Boat and Motor

One day Eino and Teivo were rocking away on the front porch talking. They got to talking about things that "had turned up missing." Eino told Teivo that he had "a better one." He said, "I had a boat and motor I was going to buy stolen before I even got it! And the worse part of the whole deal was, it was stolen legally!!" Eino then went on to explain how it happened.

"Well," said Eino, "Isn't it funny how something you never had can be lost even before you get it?" We sit here thinking of all those people in high places that cannot figure out why our economy gets so slow at times. They have not been able to figure it out with all their wisdom, plus all the experts that help them (the ones you see all the time on TV telling us their opinion of why we get into the mess we get into at times). You and I, Teivo, sitting on our porch, in the old U.P. of Michigan, have our opinions, which may be just as right as theirs! I took out my little calculator the other day and with no problem at all figured out why a person does not have the money to spend that he used to have. (This is before the tax increase of 1993). When Eino retired he started getting paid just once a month so this made things a lot easier to figure out. There is no doubt that people cannot afford to go hunting and fishing like they used to, or go out and buy a motorhome or a new boat and motor, unless you want to use that plastic money. Here are Eino's figures:

They are based on what Eino was told was the average salary in a paper mill job in the U.P. at the time, $30,000.

Now, Eino was told that if you figured out the Federal tax (before 1993), then the Michigan income tax, add in your Social Security Tax, you will end up paying right around 33% of your salary. This would add up to just about $9,900 out of your $30,000 salary right off the top. It is gone before you even get to see it, but they tell you it is really yours only they go out and spend it for you. So, now I'm (Eino) at $20,100 in what we call "take home pay."

BUT!

During the year property taxes are sure to come due. (There were some interesting comments on this during the past year). Let's use an average of both taxes for the year at $1,200 (Property is not worth much in the U.P.). You take this $1,200 dollars from your take home pay of $20,100, and you have $18,900 left to play with.

BUT!

Here in Michigan, besides the income tax you have sales tax. Let's use an easy figure of $500 for this. $500 from your $18,900 leaves you with $18,400 now.

BUT!

You have to remember all the tax you pay on each gallon of gas you buy, and with my miles driven, it comes to around $350 a year. $350 from your $18,400 leaves you with a total of $18,050 left for your family to live on.

BUT!

In Michigan, our legislator says we have to pay a fee of $75.00 per car to cover all those stolen down in the big cities. Eino, with his and her cars, plus his woods truck, and license fees for the three can kiss around $330 a year good-bye here. So, $330 from his $18,050 leaves him with a total of $17,720 left to feed the wife and kids.

BUT!

A few years back, Eino moved into the city so his boy would be closer to school for sports activities. So now he has the city water and sewer tax that seems to stay the same even if you go on vacation for a month. Here you can kiss about another $800 a year good-bye. $800 from his $17,720 leaves his family with around $16,920 left. His dreams of a boat have dwindled to a used canoe.

BUT!

Up here in the U.P., you like to enjoy things out of doors, so you have to hunt and fish, own a boat and trailer, have an ORV (ATV), a snow-mobile or two, plus a hunting camp that you have to pay property taxes on. So if you figure this out, hunting licenses, fishing licenses, licenses for necessary U.P. toys, plus hunting camp taxes, there goes another $325.00 out of sight, out of mind. So, take $325 from your $16,920 and all you have left is $16,595 to feed the kids on.

BUT!

There is a federal tax built into all guns, ammo, and fishing gear, and some cities have their city tax above everything else. Then you need insurance on your home and your car, your toys, if financed, or renters' insurance if you rent. This list could go on and on. You subtract the cost of these and you have right around $15,000 or half of your money left before you even get to sit down and figure out your family budget.

The old Game Wardens used to laugh about the state coming up with a "Pick'n and Pluck'n Stamp,"(for all those of us breathing the U.P. air, looking at the U.P. scenery, or using the great Michigan out-of-doors) to cover anything and everything they may do or think of doing. It scares me how close we may be to having one of these.

Now, the bottom line is that if Eino makes $30,000 a year, he is lucky to have $15,000 to figure out how to spend on his own. Then you take in the built-in family expenses that you really have no control over, and you do not have to wonder where all your money went. It is scary as Washington and Lansing try to figure out how they can get some of the half you have left after they already took the first half. Phone bill with a tax, natural gas bill with a tax, electric bill with a tax, food bills, cloth-ing bills, family bills, and here Eino and Teivo sit on their front porch, hoping that those down in the "Big House" do not figure out any more really good deals for them! They are not sure they can afford them.

After all, they already stole Eino's boat and Teivo's motorhome before they ever got to use them! BUT, cheer up-there is always one thing we in the U.P. get "FREE" from Lansing and Washington every January-our income tax books. Remember, they were thinking of you because it has your own personal name on it.

Gill net tug, catch and game wardens

Hunting camp

Winter morning along US-2

Winter Wonderland

Snowmobile trail (engine failure)

Looking out of my deer blind

U.P. Waterfalls
Tahquamenon State Park

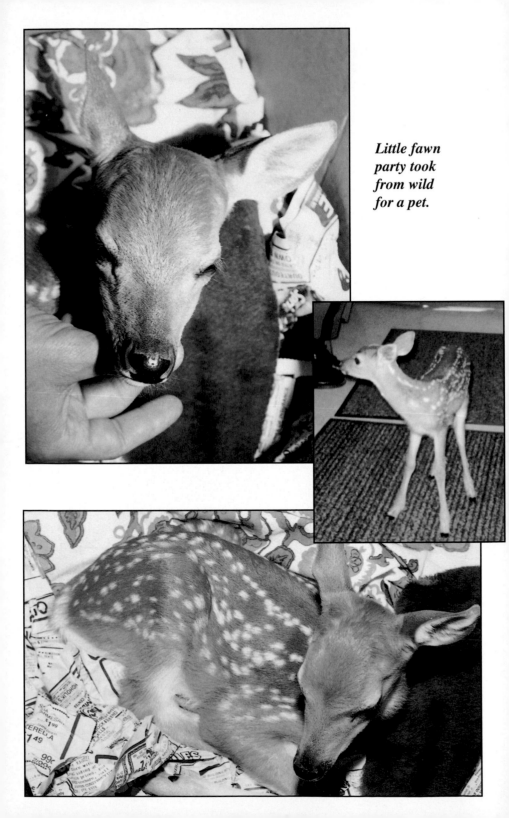

Little fawn party took from wild for a pet.

*Some of my
hunting buddies*

Lake Michigan Beach

Yooper teenagers along Lake Michigan

A morning stroll along the beach

*Could this be my
ferocious hunting dog?*

"Hon, it's your turn to shovel the drive."

"But Mom, I did shut the door."

Chapter 16
Bad Checks, Toivola Style

We all remember the days in Washington when you could write all the checks you wanted and never get those lovely little notes from your bank asking you to please deposit some money and subtract $20.00 from your new balance! Well, I just could not let this chance pass me by as I over heard Eino and Teivo trying to understand how things work in the "Big House".

I have to start out with this to try to defend the good names of all us "GUYS" out there (my wife thinks otherwise). For all these years, we have always heard the story about a wife saying, "But honey, there has to still be money in the checking account because there are still checks in my checkbook." It is really hard to take when the truth comes out that it was a "GUY" that thought this all the time! It just makes your average "Yooper" want to move right out to his deer blind and live there. Now, I understand that most all of us normal people have received those little love notes from the bank telling us we pulled a no-no and asking us to please place some money in our checking account to cover the last check we wrote. BUT! Over 800 hundred of them?! Eino has trouble with this.

Here sit Eino and Teivo in their rockers on the front porch in Toivola trying to understand Washington-type checking accounts.

Sitting and rocking, Eino and Teivo trying to balance their checkbook and figure out what might have gone wrong seeing they had just received one of those little notes from the Last Chance Bank of Toivola, which by the way has a branch in Winona. Eino says to Teivo, "We had another problem with the check I wrote at the corner store." Teivo replies, "Eino, you have to really be more careful. That makes 850 checks we have mis-under-stood so far this year. That 850 does not include the "good" ones and there had to be a few of those. Now, I'm sure there had to be some good ones in there someplace. The law of averages says that there just had to be a few that made it through with out getting red flagged! Right."

"Now Teivo, let's figure this checkbook problem out. The Last Chance Bank here in Toivola wants $20.00 for each overdraft check we write."

"Eino, that's easy to figure out. I'm sure glad they use round figures; it makes it a lot easier for us. Now, let's see, 850 bad checks times $20.00 comes to an even $17,000.00 we owe the bank."

"Round figures sure are nice to work with," Eino says.

Teivo asked,"Eino, does this mean if we pay the $17,000.00 for writing the checks we do not have to pay the money to cover the amount of the checks we wrote?"

"I'm not sure, Teivo, but that does not seem fair."

"Ya know, Teivo, it just doesn't seem right for only writing one bad check for each charge. Besides, Teivo, you remember that little sign posted at the corner store that read, "A $15.00 fee will be charged by us for all returned checks?" That means we can add another $12,750 to the $17,000 we owe the bank if we want to have good credit at the store. Let's see, this figure now has grown to $29,750 we owe somebody!"

"Ya, but Eino, remember last spring when we were sitting here figuring things out? We could buy all of Winona and half of Toivola for less than we owe the bank and corner store, then we would own them both and not have to pay ourselves back. Right?"

"Ok", says Teivo, "Let's figure this out. We owe a total of about $30,000.00 for our actions on our checking account."

"Ya, but Teivo," says Eino, "It's not our fault!! So we shouldn't have to pay!! We got lied to!!"

"How so, Eino?"

"Well, Teivo, it's like this. Remember when we went into the bank to open our joint checking account? Ya, in the Last Chance Bank branch in Winona. Well, right over the counter was this big sign that read, "FREE CHECKING!!""

"You're right, Eino, they tricked us!"

Like I said, it has nothing to do with anything, but I just had to defend the good name of us guys. Maybe, some of us are just too believing, and things are not what they always first appear to be.

Chapter 17
U.P. Vehicles

There are some real dangers about getting out of shouting distance of the U.P. It seems, no matter where you go in the U.P., you will find someone who knows someone or a friend of a friend to give you a hand if you ever have a problem. However, there are the times we have to wander away from home, and with that, there is a risk involved. These stories are about a couple of those trips away from home.

The Price of Parenting

I have to close out this year, then start next year being refreshed. This story is about going to Pensacola, Florida, 1400 miles away from home, to pick up my daughter from college. A couple weeks ago I wrote an article about my Little Red Truck, (that is another story), but come to find out, the same guy that made my truck worked on my car!! What can a person say?

We left Manistique to head down to Florida during a hard steady rain while it was so dark you would have thought it was evening at noonday. I should have known how things were going to go when before we made it to Rogers Park (only 7 miles from home), some clown in a big semi-truck almost ran us over. We regained our normal heartbeat and headed for our first stop by Milwaukee. My wife kept getting this funny feeling like a river of water running through the dash onto her legs. Now our car has never leaked like this before, but there sat my wife with a towel over her lap to keep her dry. (I guess the turbulence from the semi that tried to kill us caused the car to leak.) In fact, it got so bad that we had to force a towel up over the tape player to try to keep the water off it. The towel did not work, and the tape player still got goofy from getting wet. Water and all, we got down just south of Fond-du-lac, Wisconsin, but we kept losing speed. All of a sudden we did not have any speed at all, for the engine quit running. Thank goodness there was a place across a field where I could get a man to call for help. Out came a wrecker, and off we went.

They towed us in and got the car running, but it would not stay running. They finally found out what it was. The vacuum advance had gone out, and since it was hooked to the computer, guess what ? Wrong!! Would you believe that I own the only car in the world that has a ten and a four-teen point plug going into the computer? All other cars have a ten and a twelve!! But this guy had a mind like a U.P. garage specialist. He took a hose from the vacuum advance and stuck it on the bolt for the battery to bypass it, and off we went. We hoped! We got to the boys' and left early the next morning for the 1,100 miles left.

Only I did notice one little thing as the guy was working on my car. It seemed that there was anti-freeze running down from the head around the distributor. O' well, life goes on.

We spent the second night in Nashville after stopping at K-Mart and getting some window sealer goop so I could stand out in the rain and try to slow down the leaks to let my wife take off her life jacket. Would you believe after I did this, it did not rain the rest of the way down and back!!

We made it to Florida and just had to put a new battery and wipers on the car, and we were ready to head back. We picked my daughter up in Florida at noon Friday and hoped to make the 1,000 miles back to O'Hare airport in Chicago by noon Saturday to meet my boy, Johnny, and his wife while they had a four-hour layover there. Our other boy and his wife were coming down so we could all get together for supper. All went well, the smell of anti-freeze now and then, but the computer hooked to the battery bolt was doing great. That is, until we stopped around Crown Point, Ind. We had around one hundred miles to go before we made it to O'Hare. We ate, got gas, and started out north on 65. As we hit the four lane and stepped on the gas, the car shook so bad the exhaust pipe broke. I had this sinking feeling but found out that around 65-70 miles an hour the ride smoothed out. So guess what? I was either going to drive at 25 or 75,and it's against the law to drive 25 on an expressway. I made the best time through Chicago that I have ever made. The only problem was those toll booths. Slow down, throw in your money, get over in the side lane, and hang on til you hit seventy. We got to O'Hare, met the kids, and went out to eat. All eight adults and the dog were in my boy's car because there was no way I was driving mine except due North.

After our meal, it was buckle up, hang on, and shake for the boy's house in Wisconsin. Now have you ever had that feeling when you come off one four lane onto another doing 70 in a 55 (because if you don't you will fall apart.) on the inside lane going to merge and guess what! Guess who is in the lane next to you ! One of Wisconsin's finest. Only his car must have vibrated worse than mine for he was doing way over my seventy. We made it to my boy's and parked the car til the trip home after Christmas. We looked for parts but had no luck.

We took the two-lanes north at 25-30 miles an hour with only 300 miles to get home. We finally hit the four-lane on a downhill grade, got it up to 65, and off we went. Only now I could even feel it vibrate at this speed. We hit the Michigan-Wisconsin border and had to stop for gas. Now this you are not going to believe !! We started out hanging onto our coffee ready to hit 25 miles an hour and feel the shaking start. We hit 25, then 35, then 50, then 55, and it did not shake ! It did not shake the rest of the way home! I guess it just needed some of the good U.P. air running through it.

So, if you see a hanket once riding around in a little brown car, now you know why. Plus, Rhonda somehow had to get back to school in January. UPS maybe??

Thank Goodness For Golfers

This story really took place before the last one, but somehow the one above jarred my memory back to this story. It seems like people like to hear about the interesting trips a person can get involved in when they leave the safety of the U.P.

The other day a couple of us were talking at coffee about getting a loan from a bank these days. The way things are now-a-days, you have to sign forty-seven papers and fill out twenty-seven forms starting with what boat your ancestors came over to America on or if they were here all the time. Then, you have three days to change your mind. But, it was not always this way in the "Good Old Days".

During a trip I took, I was on my way down to Missouri to visit my wife's family. On this trip, we had my two boys, my mother, my brother Tim, and the wife and I (Rhonda was two months shy of being officially with us.) We went down through lower Michigan, through Lansing, then down toward Coldwater on the border with Indiana, on Interstate 69. We got south of Lansing, almost to Marshall, when the car decided it was getting too hot and wanted a rest. We called a wrecker and had it towed into Marshall to be fixed. The party at the garage got it running again, for a fee, and off we went. It was now late in the evening, but we were on our way again, for another forty miles before the car died again. This time we were near Coldwater. We already knew it was going to be real expensive to get it on the road again. Besides, I was getting a little "gun-shy" of wanting it to go to Missouri with us. So, we parked it at a garage and walked across the road to a motel for the night.

The next morning, I called the local Conservation Officer that worked the Coldwater area because when I was a Fire Officer for the DNR in the Thumb area of Michigan, I worked with this officer. In fact, when he moved to Coldwater, I took his place as a Conservation Officer in the Tuscola County area in lower Michigan. I told him where we were and told him about the car problems we were having. I asked his advice about car dealers in the area seeing he lived there. He came by and took the wife, my two boys, and my brother out to his house while my mom and I looked for a car.

Now, it was a Saturday morning and almost all the car dealers were going to close at noon, so we had to move fast. We looked at a number of cars and ended up at a Chevy dealer in Coldwater. After looking at a number of used cars, we found a new car that seemed like the best deal for the price (at least a new car ought to get us to Missouri and back).

You have to remember, we were hundreds of miles from home, hoping to buy a new car, and with only one little problem - they wanted money for it! Needless to say I did not have that kind of money with me or anywhere else. Plus, back then in the area where I lived, the banks were not open on Saturday. So, what's a body to do ? Since it was now near 11:30 am and the car dealer closed at noon, I had to do something. Being from a small town where everybody knew everybody else, I asked the car dealer if I could use his phone? After he gave me the ok, I called the home of the man from the bank I usually dealt with. (In fact, his wife worked for the District Court in the county I worked, so we knew each other real well.) The wife answered the phone, and I asked her if her husband was home and told her my problem. She said, "No, he just left for the golf course, but if you call him right away you should catch him at the clubhouse. He would not have had time to start playing yet seeing he just left home."

I hung up the phone and called the golf course right away and asked for my banker. When he came to the phone, I told him where I was and the problem I had. The banker was told I had found a new car that I felt was the best deal I could find for the price. I also told him, as usual, I did not have any money.

He asked me, "Do you have your checkbook with you?" I told him I did. He told me, "Just go ahead and write a check out for the amount of the car, and when you get home, we'll make out loan papers on it." I told him I was just starting out on vacation, and it would be three weeks before I got back. He told me that would not be a problem and asked to speak to the car dealer. My banker asked the car dealer if he would accept my personal check for a new car if he gave him (the car dealer) his word over the phone that the bank would stand behind the check. The Chevy dealer said that this would not be a problem and took my check, on the banker's word, and we drove off in a brand new car to continue our vacation. A car paid for with a check from a checking account with no money in it on a stranger's word from a golf course.

You just have to remember that things were done that way years ago. A man's word was his bond for a loan, and when he gave his word, it meant something.

The interesting, untold part of the story was that we went from a full sized Buick wagon to a Chevy Vega wagon loaded with six people and all our gear. Oh, well. We had a great time down in Missouri on vacation with my mom and brother.

Old U.P.
logging
pictures
from
Dad's stuff

Chapter 18
Yooper English

Well, I guess I'll just have to take a chapter and help some of you out there understand how life really is. You need to realize that when telling a story in a deer camp or on a fishing trip you do not worry about the proper use of the English language. In fact, there are some of us who, even if we did want to worry about the proper use of the English language, it would not do us a whole lot of good. It seems that no matter how hard we try someone is always changing the rules on us. We were taught that "ain't" ain't a word, but now "ain't" is a word. We were told "kids" were baby sheep not children, now they are both baby sheep AND children. We were taught that blue and green never go together, now anything and everything goes together. We were taught that you went to school to learn and that sports were extra-curricular activities. Now we find out that sports are in first place in a lot of cases and learning has been moved back to second place.

Since it is just hard for a guy out of the Stone Age to figure something out, I had to sit my daughters down and explain proper U.P. English to them - with the help of Eino and Teivo.

Then-Than-or is it Than-Then?

Well, I got a real scare the other day! I heard that they were going to use my book, "A Deer Gets Revenge", in an English literature class! Now, I figured that I was really in trouble, because I would have to come out of retirement to explain the English language as properly used in the U.P. to the students. Since I did not want to have to do this, I thought I would explain it in this chapter. I will take time to prove to all you edumacated readers my point about the proper use of English for a Yooper.

My wife and kids keep telling me the words "then" and "than" are two different words that mean different things! But, I keep telling them they are the same word just spelled different to help kids out in a spelling bee. (I used to get a lot of rest time during these back in Ontonagon grade school.) The two words are really interchangeable, let me explain.

Eino is down at the Manistique River fishing for those big salmon that run up out of Lake Michigan. He thought he hooked one but found out it was a snag and lost his last lure. So he yells over to Teivo that he is going to run down to Top-of-the-Lakes Sporting Goods for some more hooks. Off Eino goes, down to the store and buys a half dozen more lures. He is chilled from the fall weather, so then he walks across the street to a restaurant for a hot cup of coffee.

Meantime back at the river, Teivo hooks a big one!! He plays it for awhile, but cannot land it without Eino there to help with the landing net. Finally the salmon gets into the fast water and heads downstream back to the safety of Lake Michigan. Teivo not only loses his temper, but his hook and all the line off his spool. So, he takes a walk up the sidewalk to the Holiday Station Store where they sell some fishing gear. He buys his fishing gear, than walks up to meet Eino and have a cup of coffee.

Now let me prove my point on proper English.

1) Were not both Eino and Teivo fishing in the Manistique River? Yes!

2) Did not both Eino and Teivo lose their fishing gear? Yes!

3) Did not both Eino and Teivo go to a sporting goods place and get new gear? Yes!

4) Now, did not both Eino and Teivo walk across the street and end up having a hot cup of coffee? Yes!

So, my case is proven!! Both words worked and were interchangeable in their use seeing both Eino and Teivo had some hot coffee.

Not a Word?

Now, one other time I used the word "flustrated" in a story, and my daughter informed me, "Dad, there is no such word as flustrated!" I said there had to be, and I told her this story to prove it.

Your brother, Rob, that lives down in middle Wisconsin gets off work around midnight November 14th. He is three hundred miles from home, and firearm deer season opens at daylight the next morning. He rushes home from work to pick up his wife and head for the Promised Land of the U.P.

He drives all night through ice and snow, gets run off the road by a vehicle, and a party in a 4x4 stops and pulls him out. There is sleet and snow all three hundred miles, but they make it home around 5:30 a.m. Mom has breakfast ready, so he eats and changes before we make a fast trip to our deer blinds. As we go out into the yard to our hunting vehicle, we find it has a flat tire. After we work up a sweat changing the tire, we fly out to our deer blinds. I drop him off at his and head for mine.

Your brother must have dozed off, because when he looked down the hill to his bait pile, there stood a nice buck. Once it dawned on him that a buck was standing there, he pulled up and shot to fast, and missed the first buck he had ever missed! The buck took off, and your brother looked around in the fog and the rain to see if he had lucked out and hit it. When he shot, the deer flipped right over backwards, so just maybe.... No luck, so he started out to get me from my blind to help him look because there was no snow on the ground to help him see tracks.

As he starts up the hill from his bait pile, he looks at his scope and sees that it is all fogged up and wet. Forget it! He has shot twice, tramped all over the place, and he is just going to head out and find Dad!

He takes about a half dozen steps behind his blind when up jumps the biggest buck he has ever seen in the woods!!! He pulls up to shoot, but cannot find the buck in his wet, fogged-up scope before it gets into the trees!! NOW HE WAS FLUSTRATED!!

I said, "Honey, you have never been there, or you would realize there is too such a word."

Now, these and other valuable facts on the English language come from a guy that spent two hours in Mr. Klein's Latin class (back when Latin was offered in high school.) That was before he realized that Latin could cause serious brain damage to the average Ontonagon teenager and dropped out to take an extra hour of gym.

1st - 2nd - 3rd Person

Well, my daughter got to go back to college in Florida the other day for a rest. (What other daughter spends her vacation reading over Dad's crazy fish report stories?) My daughter has the hardest time trying to get Dad to understand that you can't use the 1st person (I-me-we), right along with the 2nd person (you) and throw in a 3rd person or two (he-she-they). They just don't mix and belong together, I guess? Since I always try to take time with my kids when they don't understand something, I just told her she does not have the right outlook on things.

You see, I told her, a Game Warden just has a different outlook on things than a normal person does. Not saying that Game Wardens are abnormal! A Game Warden's thinking just runs along different lines. You see, when a Game Warden thinks and hears about a 1st, 2nd and 3rd person it goes like this.

It is a cool clear night on Thompson Creek or any other creek in the U.P. The steelhead trout may be running, and salmon are running upstream to spawn, also. With all this bait in the creek, the Game Wardens plan a patrol to go in after dark and check things out. As they look around the area, they spot a pickup truck hidden back in the trees. The Game Wardens hide the patrol unit and walk back toward the weir on the creek. Their walking is done in the dark without the use of any flashlights. As they near the weir on the creek, using only the moonlight to see, they have to watch out for the "1st person". Now, this "1st person" is usually the lookout for any Game Wardens that may be walking into the creek. The "1st person" is going to be a little ways off from the creek along the trails leading into the area where the fish are spawning so he can yell and warn his buddies if he spots a Game Warden. This is the "1st person".

If the Game Warden is lucky enough to work his way around the "1st person", he now has to watch for the "2nd person". This is the poacher that is working his way along the bank of the creek with a light trying to spot some fish to let his buddy the "3rd person", who is the violator in the creek with a spear, so he can spear the fish. I told my daughter that a Game Warden is used to working around the 1st, 2nd, and 3rd person, and if he is lucky enough, he catches all three, and they all go to court together-no matter what order you grab them in. Somehow she still does not get the picture the way a Game Warden does.

Now I tell her, "It is a cool clear fall night and two Game Wardens are on patrol in the Cooks area. The Game Warden and his partner are sitting near a field where some deer are feeding. All of a sudden, they observe a vehicle coming down the road towards the field where the deer are feeding. While the people in the vehicle are using a spotlight to try and locate the deer, the officers pull out of their hiding spot without any headlights on and come up behind the car that is doing the shining. The Game Warden reaches down and pulls on the headlights, flips on the spotlight to shine into the back window of the car, and turns on the blue light to stop them! Then and only then does a Game Warden worry about a 1st, 2nd, or 3rd person!"

You see, the "1st person" is the driver of the vehicle that was shining, the "2nd person" is the party that was using the spotlight to try and locate the deer feeding out in the field, and the "3rd person" is the poacher sitting in the back seat with the window down holding a rifle to shoot at the deer when person number 2 shines them. Now, a Game Warden worries about party number 3 (with a firearm) after party number 1, but before party number 2.

After I take the time to explain all these 1st, 2nd, and 3rd party facts to her, she says she must be going to learn that next semester at college because she definitely never learned it yet.

Seriously, the stories in my books are just to enjoy and get a laugh out of. The key to good story telling, is to re-tell them exactly as they were or are told to you.

The crew of the 60's

Backwoods Glossary

Up here in the Great North Woods, there is a tendency to use terms or phrases to make a point. To some of you, they may be used in a way you never realized they could be. Other words or terms, you may just have not had the opportunity to ever use. This Backwoods Glossary is to help you out in understanding why we talk like we do.

U.P. (Upper Michigan): If, for some strange reason, you have never traveled in Michigan, these two letters would seem strange to you. First, understand that Michigan has two peninsulas- the upper and lower. The lower peninsula is made up of two parts, Lower Michigan and Northern Michigan. But, the really important part of Michigan lies across the Mackinac Bridge. This part of Michigan is called the U.P., for the Upper peninsula of Michigan. The people up here in the U.P. live in their own little world and like it that way. The only problem is that most of the laws are passed down in Lower Michigan to correct their problems, then they effect us, who may not even be part of that problem. Some of the Big City folks that pass these laws never have learned to understand and love the U.P. like we that live here do. The natives of the U.P. have trouble understanding the "why-for" about some of these laws, therefore they feel they really must not apply to them.

Two of the biggest industries in the U.P. are paper mills and the men that work in the woods suppling trees to these mills so they can produce their product. There are probably more colleges in the U.P., per capita, than anywhere else in the country. But even with this, there are still a lot of natives up here that feel you could sure ruin a good person if you sent them to one of these colleges. News of a serious crime will travel from one side of the U.P. to the other like a wild fire. Because most people up here are not used to it. To them, serious crimes are when someone takes a deer or some fish illegally and is dumb enough to get caught. They don't even take these crimes to seriously unless the poacher should step over the line and get to greedy.

Sports teams that play teams from other towns in the U.P. always seem to have relatives, or friends, on the other team. Everyone knows someone, or someone that married someone, that knew someone from over there. To win a state championship, you have to beat those teams from "down state". To do this is a dream come true for any red-blooded U.P. boy or girl.

When I was growing up, we had only had part-time radios. So we had to be Green Bay (Wisconsin) Packer and Milwaukee Brave fans. As a boy living in the Western U.P., we could not pick up any radio stations that carried broadcast of the teams from Lower Michigan. For this reason, we grew up feeling that we were a state unto ourselves. We could not be part of Michigan, because it was just to far away, and the only way to get there was by boat. We knew we were not part of Wisconsin, so we were just the Good Old U.P.!

Up here in the U.P., where life is tough, but things are good, and it is just a great place to live.

Some backwoods (U.P.) terms:

2-TRACK: (roads)

The U.P. has hundreds of miles of this type of road. All these roads consist of are two tire ruts worn into the ground from all the vehicle travel throughout the years. Usually you have a high, grass-covered center and mud holes in the low spots. This is one of the reasons that so many people in the U.P. feel you cannot live without a 4x4 pickup. These roads are never worked on or improved and you get what you see.

Blacktop Roads:

These are the 2-tracks, that are worse than unimproved roads. They are covered by mud or clay and it is a real trick to stay between the trees on some of these. There are also a lot of these type roads for which the U.P. is famous. Many a fishermen or hunter has spent hours and hours trying to get out of one of these blacktop roads, usually after you misjudged what you were getting into. Two of the first things I learned after becoming a Game Warden stationed in the U.P. were: It's hard to get 2-ton stuck at fifty miles an hour, so wind it up and keep moving. The other one follows point one, you are never really stuck till you stop. In other words, if one of these blacktop areas sneak up on you, floor it and don't stop 'til you reach high ground or hit something unmovable.

Poachers:

These are not people that cook eggs in hot water, but may get themselves in hot water now and then. They are outlaws that rob the honest hunters and fishermen of their chance to get game and fish legally. In years past, it was a way of life in the U.P. that was passed down from generation to generation. When it was an accepted thing to do, the Game Warden not only had a hard time catching the poachers, but he usually had an even harder time trying to get a conviction in the local courts.

Shining:

(Shinning, Shining, Shiners), Shiners are the poachers that use a spot-light to look for deer at night, in order to shoot them. Until the fines got to high, it was the way that a lot of the outlaws did their hunting here in the U.P. They would take a pair of spotlights, hook them up in their vehi-cle, then drive around while casting the rays of the spotlights out into fields or an old orchards, until they spotted a deer. The deer, blinded by the bright light, would stand there staring at the light while the poacher got out his gun and shot it. There is really no sport in it, because it is so deadly. You will notice I spelled shinning, with two "n's" at times. Well, I did this on my tickets for dozens of cases throughout the years, until a State Trooper told me it was spelled wrong. He said it should only have one "n", so on the next couple tickets I changed how I spelled shining. You see for years, when I caught someone hunting deer at night with a spotlight, the only thing I would write for a charge on the ticket was the one word "shinning". With the one word spelled, Shinning, they knew what they did, I knew what they had done, and most important the aver-age U.P. Judge knew what they were standing before him for doing. Well, the first time I caught a crew out spotlighting for deer and put shin-ing (with one n) on their ticket they pled "Not Guilty". They must have been confused by the spelling and so was I.

Spearers:

These are people that have a way of taking fish with the use of a spear. The spear can have from three to five prongs, with pointed tips, these prongs have barbs on the end to hold the fish on the spear after they spear it. Now in some areas, it is legal to spear certain types of non-game fish. The problem the Game Warden has is with those that spear trout, salmon, walleye, etc. or "game fish". When these fish come into real shallow water to spawn, a Game Warden will spend hour after hour watching the fish spawning in these areas.

Extractors:

This is a term for those illegal fishermen that may come along a creek with a spear trying to extract the spawning fish from the creek. They may use other devices besides a spear. For instance a weighted hook, hand nets, their hands, etc.

Gill Netters:

These are people, both legal and illegal, that use a gill net to take fish. In some areas, there is a commercial fishery allowed with the use of gill nets, but in Michigan it is never legal for "sport" fishermen to use a gill net to take fish. A gill net is made up of nylon string in little squares (it looks something little a small woven wire fence) built so the fish will swim into the net putting their head through the square openings. Then, they get caught when their larger body will not fit through the squares and their gills keep them from backing out of the nets. I have observed illegal gill net fishermen take hundreds of pounds of steelhead in a couple of hours, if they set their gill nets in the right spot.

Fishhouse or fish shed:

In areas of the U.P., along the great lakes where there is a legal commercial fishery, most of those business involved have a building where they clean, box in ice, and store their catch. They may also repair their nets in this building. On account of the smell around a full time commercial fishing operation, most of these sheds are located away from any residence. They also may be on the river bank where the commercial fisherman ties up his fish tug. For this reason they are often used for illegal activity, sometimes by others than those that own them.

Deer camp:

A deer camp can be any type of building used for offering protection from the elements. It is also used to get-a-way from home during the hunting season. Some are as nice as any house, better than some, while others may be made out of plastic, heavy paper, scrap lumber, or anything to keep the weather out. The following rules are some of the usual type that are proper for deer camp life.

(1) You cannot shave or take a bath, no matter how many days you may be staying at camp. You are allowed to wash your face and hands. But this is your own choice, You do not have to if you do not want to. This is one reason young boys love to go to deer camp with Dad.

(2) There is no proper way to dress while at deer camp, if it feels good wear it! You can even wear the same clothes all week long. This includes your socks, if you can catch them after the first three days at camp.

(3) The "menu" is always made up of all the "proper" things that you cannot afford to eat all the rest of the year at home. Both good and bad for you.

(4) It is never wrong to tell a "true" story on another camp member. Remembering it is of more value if you can dress it up a little to make him suffer all the time you are telling it. During the telling of his misfor-

tune we must all remember that we will all pay for our mistakes, sooner or later, if and when our hunting "buddies" find out about them.

(5) It is a crime, punishable by banishment, to talk about school, or school work, or any work for that matter while at deer camp.

(6) You can throw, hang or just leave your socks and clothes any where they land when you remove them. You can hang your wet socks from anything that has something to hang them from to try and dry them out before the next days hunt. Always remembering it is "most" important to have dry socks by daybreak the next morning.

(7) What may be called work at home is not work at deer camp. Therefore getting things done at deer camp is not classified as work, but a team effort. For this reason, it is not wrong for a boy to do dishes, sweep a floor, pick up trash (that he missed getting in the trash can when he threw it that way, with one of his famous hook shots), or even do what Dad asks him to do, the first time Dad asks him to do it.

You would have to spend a week at a real U.P. deer camp to really know the true feeling of being a U.P. deer hunter. With these easy-to-apply rules, you can see why deer camp life is so important to a boy during his informative teenage years. It is really important that a young man start out with a proper perspective on life.

Big House:

This is the Michigan State Capital, from some areas of the U.P. it can be over 400 miles away. In Lansing, this is where "they" compile all the rules and ideas that are put out to confuse the average hunter or fisherman, while out in the field. It is the feeling of a lot of U.P. sportsmen, that most of those that work down there, in Lansing's Big House, never in their lives set foot in the real out-of-doors, or wet a line in a back woods stream. What they know, they got from someone that wrote a book without ever having set their feet in a real woods, or having gone back woods fishing either. It is just passed on from desk to desk, year after year, put into volumes of rules and law books that we out in the field have to learn to live with. This while trying to enjoy ourselves out in the real Northwoods, the U.P.

Wifee:

(W-IF-EE; wily) This is one's wife. To pronounce it right, you say the "W" sound, then the "IF", than draw out the "EE".

Big Lake:

This can be any of the Great Lakes that border Michigan. Instead of say-ing, "I went fishing out on Lake Michigan Saturday". A native from the U.P. would say, "I went fishing on the Big Lake Saturday afternoon".

Off road vehicles:

ATV'S, ORV'S, dirt bikes, etc. These may be any of the type vehicles that are made primary to operate off a improved road. Some may be home made, while other are sold by dealers. In the U.P. you will find a lot of these used by sportsmen to get around when hunting and fishing.

Game Wardens:

Conservation Officer, C.O.'s, and Game Wardens are all one and the same, up here in the U.P. They have been around for better than 100 years serving the people of Michigan. The stories they can tell and those told on them are told over and over around the U.P. This is how my newspaper, story telling got started.

Backwoods Glossary

Chapter II

Holiday Stations:

Holiday? Here, in Michigan's U.P., you always hear the expression, "I'm going to stop by Holiday on the way". Some of you folks may not under-stand what a Holiday is and how far advanced the U.P. is over other areas of our country. I'll try to explain. Holiday, here in the north coun-try, is a gas station-store. The Holiday Stations have been around for years and years, and in the U.P. they are like a mini-mall. The U.P. and Holiday were way ahead of the rest of the world on this idea of doing all your shopping in one stop. Get your gas plus whatever else you may need here at Holiday.

Sometimes it just takes awhile for you all to catch up to us, Yoopers.

Years ago, when Christmas time rolled around, you went down to the Holiday to do your Christmas shopping. It had a great toy selection, in fact, in most U.P. towns the best to be found. If company dropped in for a surprise visit and you needed food items, off you went to Holiday to get what you needed. When hunting and fishing season rolled around, they put out a paper and sales ad to get you into Holiday to fill your needs-everything from guns and ammo, to poles, hooks, and line. If you snagged your waders off, you went to Holiday for new ones. If your feet got cold out deer hunting, off to Holiday for warm foot gear. If your motorized deer blind broke down on a weekend, off to the auto parts section of Holiday to get what you needed. What am I saying? Before the rest of the world was smart enough to think about putting other than gas and oil supplies in their gas stations Holiday was there. Now they have moved up one more step because most Holiday Stations have copies of my books for sale.

Remember when traveling through the U.P., if a town does not have a Holiday station, keep on trucking til you find one because that town you are in has not arrived yet!

Copper Country:

In so many parts of my book, you will read about things that took place in the Copper Country. This area covers what is called the Keweenaw Peninsula over to the area of the copper mines to the west. Those of us that lived in the Copper Country felt you were going into the world of the great unknown if you left Ontonagon, Houghton, Baraga, or Keweenaw County. In fact, a person growing up when I did may have left the Copper Country for the first time when he went into the service. The Copper Country is really a melting pot of people from all over the world. When I was growing up, it was nothing for some of the old folks not being able to speak English; they talked in their native language. In fact, one of the things that really bugged a teenage boy from the Copper Country was when there were a couple of girls your buddy and you wanted to get to know, and they would talk back and forth in Finnish, and we did not have the foggiest idea what they were saying. The history of the Copper Country is both interesting and unreal if you study it. A person could move away and be gone for years, but when asked where they are from, they always answer the Copper Country.

In the Copper Country, everybody knows somebody that knows somebody else. When on a radio show talking about my first book, "A Deer Gets Revenge", a party called in and wanted to know if I was Harry Theiler's grandson. Then another party called in and wanted to know if I was Tim Walker's brother. (Tim is my brother that lives in a home in Hancock, MI, in the Copper Country). Copper Country people are special people that help make up a place called the U.P. where people know and care about each other. Come visit the U.P. and Copper Country someday, and you will see what I mean.

The other day:

I keep telling my kids and the readers of my newspaper article that when I use the saying, "The other day", it could mean anytime between birth and death. It is up to the person you are talking to, try and figure out what era you are talking about. Up here in the U.P., a party could start to tell you a hunting story by saying, " The other day a buddy and I...." and the story may have taken place back in the forties. (1940's) You have to remember that good stories never really get old; they just get better and added to in the telling of them. There was one officer I worked with- could he tell stories! He would get going into a story and you would sit there and listen. Pretty soon bits and pieces would start to ring a bell. Then all of a sudden it would dawn on you that you were with him when "his story" took place, but you really never remembered it happening like he was telling it, or could it have?

One of my boys called me from college a while back (another one of those time means nothing U.P. phrases) to ask me about the history of the 60's. This was for a paper he had to do for a history course. I told him, "Son, the 60's do not qualify as history yet.That is when your dad says, you know the other day, or awhile back, and that makes it today time not history time."

Exspurt:

Sometimes in the U.P. we have our own way of spelling and understanding things. Here is one of those terms.

I have a buddy that is a U.P. potato farmer. (You have to really wonder about anybody that tries to farm in the U.P.) But this buddy has a great definition for all those exspurts that rule down in the Big House. It is one of those terms you have to think about, but the more you think about it, the more you feel that this potato farmer may go down in history as a great U.P. philosopher. We will get talking about all those rules and laws the exspurts down in Lansing and Washington pass that are totally unreal, and my buddy will say, "Always remember that an ex-spurt is only a drip under pressure!" Now, I wonder.....

But then,you have all these TV shows on how with an outdoor exspurt on just about everything. Let's be real now. Do they ever get skunked out there fishing? Do you ever see them spending all day baiting hooks for the kids and getting the kids' lines untangled? Or they get the boat unloaded and the motor won't start? Somehow, someway, I get the feeling these exspurts have never hunted or fished out there in the real world. Let me give you an example of an exspurt.

One night I happened to be going through the cable channels and came across this exspurt fisherman who had his own TV show. It happened that on this show he was fishing an area off Lake Superior that I was in charge of, so I decided to watch his show. Here is our exspurt telling people how it should be done and where the nice steelhead fishing is in the U.P. As I watched, I couldn't believe it. So I got on the phone and called a Conservation Officer that worked for me and worked the area in the program.

I told him, "John, you blew it and missed one." He replied, "You must be watching the same program I am watching." Then we both had a good laugh. Why? Because here was this exspurt going along a trout stream running out of Lake Superior with an illegal device used to take trout in the spring of the year in that area! I told John, "Maybe we ought to send him a ticket in the mail. We have what he's doing on film, and he is even telling us he's doing it." But you have to understand that this fishing exspurt was a "troll" (a person that lives below the Big Mac Bridge.), and therefore, you get what you pay for. Now, remember what an exspurt is, "A drip under pressure", and life will be a lot easier to understand.

Huskavarina edumacation:

There has always been a feeling that there is more wisdom learned at the back end of a chain saw then what you learn in college. The more some of us see and hear what is going on in our country, the more we have to wonder. It was always an amazement to those that worked out in the field for the government to see someone go off to the "Big House" on a promotion and forget everything they learned out in the field in the first six months they were there! In fact, some of us always felt that about halfway down through the lower peninsula there was an invisible force field that made up a brain sucking machine, and by the time they passed through this going to the "Big House", they were useless to us living in the U.P.

We used to suggest that everyone after about a year or two down in Lansing's or Washington's "Big House" ought to have to spend six month back in the woods on the working end of a chain saw to get the feeling for how the real world lives again. That is why the U.P. is a special place, because from the woods, to the mines, to the papers mills, most of its people have a Husavarina Edumacation. Sometimes I think it makes them special people as you can see by some of my stories.

Bugs:

Back when I was a kid, a bug was not an insect. It was something you rode in going hunting. (look at the picture in the books of us hunting in the 40's and 50's, and you will see our Bug.) You would take an old Model T and put oversize tires on it to raise it up off the ground. Then you would find some old tire chains. Most of the time they had nobody left on them, and you were to hang on for dear life when you came to a big mud hole. A party always had this saying, "It's hard to get two ton stuck at fifty miles an hour, but when you do you are really stuck." I always said, "You are never stuck till you stop, so the key is never to stop till you hit high ground again." These vehicles were used by all the hunters back before anyone ever heard of a 4x4 pickup. They were homemade, and you were really someone when you had one. In fact I cannot count the times we gave the Game Warden a ride back into the back country when he had something to check on because he was not lucky enough to own a "Bug". But, now if a person was to make one and try to use it, they would end up having to hire a secretary to file the nine thousand-four hundred-seventy-five million tickets you would receive for having this dangerous vehicle back in the woods. Man, those were the good old days; No ORV laws, no snowmobile laws, about half the hunting laws, and no Big Mac bridge to let all those idealists across into God's country.

Yooper:

Have you ever been asked, "What's a Yooper?" It seems that there are certain terms that the real world has not got to use yet. If you take the Upper Penisula of Michigan abbreviated name "The U.P. and sound it out what do you get? It has to be the word Yooper. Therefore all the good people (natives only) that make their homes in the U.P. of Michigan have to be Yoopers. Right?

Up here in Yooper Country we have our own jokes, our own Yooper singing groups, our own terms, and a great life style.

The one thing that you want to remember is that you are born a True Yooper. It cannot be bought, you cannot get it by living here for years and years, you must be born a Yooper. We have a real problem with Troles (Those that live below the Big Mac Bridge.) coming up to Yooper land and trying to act like or become one of us, it just cannot be done! You either have it or you don't. You can come see us, we are glad when you spend your money here, we like you for a friend, but remember when you leave Yooper Land you leave as you came, not as a Yooper.